SILENT SCREAMS OF A SURVIVOR

SILENT SCREAMS OF A SURVIVOR
A Polish-American Boy's Holocaust

Mitch Garwolinski
and
Bob Hoffman

Acorn Publishing
A Division of Development Initiatives

SILENT SCREAMS OF A SURVIVOR
A Polish-American Boy's Holocaust

© 2004 Mitch Garwolinski & Bob Hoffman

Published by Acorn Publishing
A Division of Development Initiatives
P.O. Box 84, Battle Creek, Michigan 49016-0084

All rights reserved. This book, or any parts thereof, may not be duplicated in any way without the expressed written consent of its author or publisher. The information contained herein is for the personal use of the reader and may not be incorporated in any commercial programs, other books, databases or any kind of software without the written consent of the publisher or the author. Making copies of this publication, or any portions, is a violation of United States copyright laws. The only exception is brief quotations in printed reviews.

Cover artwork © 2004 Mitch Garwolinski

Printed in the United States of America
First Edition, 2004

Library of Congress Cataloging-in-Publication Data

Garwolinski, Mitchell, 1932-
  Silent screams of a survivor : a Polish-American boy's Holocaust / Mitchell Garwolinski and Bob Hoffman.-- 1st ed.
    p. cm.
  ISBN 0-9728969-6-1 (pbk.)
  1. World War, 1939-1945--Prisoners and prisons, German. 2. Garwolinski, Mitchell, 1932- 3. World War, 1939-1945--Personal narratives, Polish. 4. Polish Americans--Biography. 5. World War, 1939-1945--Concentration camps--Poland. 6. World War, 1939-1945--Atrocities--Poland. I. Hoffman, Robert Lee, 1950- II. Title.

D805.P7G364 2004
940.53'18'092--dc22

2004013550

For current information about all releases by Acorn Publishing, visit our web site: http://www.acornpublishing.com

To my sister, Irene,
and my parents
who helped me to survive against all odds.

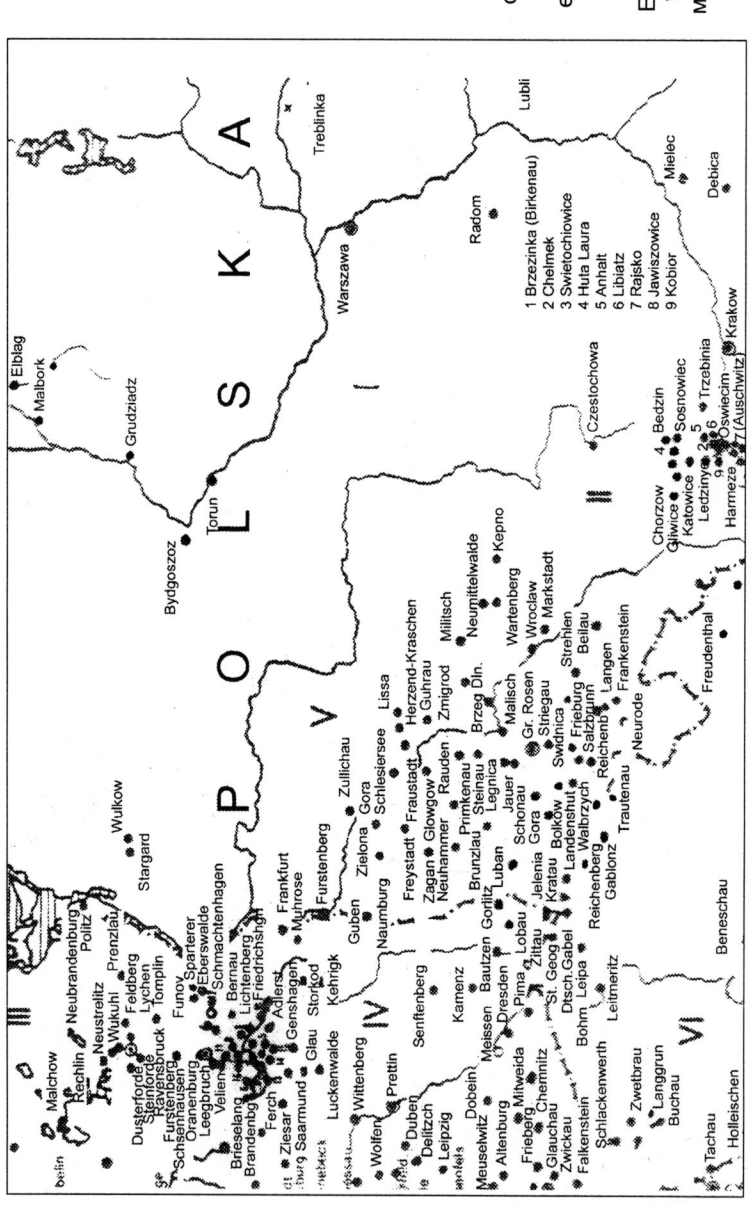

Some of the hundreds of Nazi concentration camps established in Poland and throughout Europe during World War II. Map adapted from R. Höss

Prologue

HATE: A word that speaks volumes in its four letters. Listen as you say it aloud. Does it resonate? What images does it conjure? Are they pleasant? No? Then come and hear my story of hate and love and devastation and survival. Perhaps, my words can help to light the darkness and serve as an important reminder that we all harbor the roots of hate in our existence and only by understanding hate's nature can we hope to stave it from our lives.

LISTEN: In 1937 in the town of Baranowo in the old country of Poland, we see hate—simple, destructive, and as damning to those who are its originators, as to those whose reactions can be nothing less than a feeling returned in kind. Can you see them? I can. All of these images are with me and coloring my world as I continue to walk through my life. My name is Mitchell Garwolinski and this is my story.

SEE: A teeming marketplace whose tables are surrounded with local vendors and residents. All have come to buy and sell produce, food, and everyday necessities. On this long-forgotten Monday in a place far away, an elderly couple are riding high on a wagon pulled by a single horse. The man guides the horse through the narrow streets. The soft clip clop echoes off the buildings. But this sound is soon lost in the noises emanating from the market. Nothing remarkable to see, just one glimpse of everyday rural life. The couple are seated on the rough seat of the wagon; the man wearing the long beard and black frock coat is Jewish. He holds the reins loosely. The horse has often completed this route and simply plods along. The couple's wooden crates of ducks, geese, and chickens are piled high on the wagon and dwarf them as they enter the town.

FEEL: The sun shining and the festive aura surrounding the marketplace. The couple is full of hope. Maybe, they will sell all they have for a good price. Maybe, the day will end gloriously as they return to the farm satisfied. But their optimism is tempered by the knowledge that there have been many incidents of Jews being harassed in this town. So, whatever positive expectations they may have are girded with a fear of those who hate. In their minds, it is almost impossible to conceive of such heinous activities. But the thought lingers.

HEAR: A man. He is ordering four young thugs toward the slowly moving wagon. In a plan conceived beforehand, the four young men move to one side of the wagon and grasp the wheels. The wagon stops and the woman moves closer to her husband. He says something to them, but his words are lost in the din coming from the marketplace. Grasping the wheels, the young men push the wagon up and over, and it crashes to the ground.

The old man and woman are thrown to the hard ground and injured. Their cages tumble and break open. Birds squawk and fly everywhere. The horse, now frightened beyond measure, bolts, dragging the wagon along the cobblestone street spilling the rest of its cargo. The four young men, not satisfied, begin to laugh derisively at the elderly couple laying in a heap on the road. From my perch in the window of my house, I watch as a brave onlooker runs to the horse and grasps the reins, preventing it from dragging the wagon into the crowded marketplace. As the horse stops, the tension of the moment lessens.

UNDERSTAND: My mother moves behind me and looks at the scene. "Momma, there's that man again!"

"I know. He condemns the Jews and sends his maid to

their store under cover of darkness, because he will not deal with them personally."

"Dad, what about that man?" I asked.

"He ordered the men to do this."

"Why?"

SILENCE: What can my father say? How can he explain hate to a five-year-old? What words can explain that which he does not understand himself. He does not answer, but moves closer to the window as he recognizes his father. My grandfather is a tall, strong man, and he moves to the pitifully sobbing woman. My grandfather gently picks up the injured woman and carries her to the side of the road to rest. Seeing that she is as comfortable as possible, he returns to the street and assists the man to sit by his wife. The four young hoodlums, feeling their work was complete, melt into the crowd. The man, his face glowering, moves toward my grandfather in a menacing manner. My grandfather rises to his full height and glares at him. No words are exchanged, but my grandfather's communication is clear.

WATCH: My father rushes from the window to the door and into the street. Not many people would take a chance to go against my grandfather, especially those who knew him. But with the instigator, there were five of them. My momma moves close to the window. She is trembling.

"Mr. Tszaskoma, why?" My father asks.

The man does not answer, but searches the crowd furtively for his young cohorts. Not seeing them, he begins to slow his advance. My father moves close to my grandfather, they stand together. The man turns and walks away.

Some of the men from town gather alongside the wagon and working together, right it once more. The birds—though not all of them—are gathered and placed in their cages and loaded on the wagon. I feel my mother's arm encircling me and drawing me close to her.

Just one more hate-inspired incident, in a long line of hate-inspired incidents, in a small Polish town in a time between the Great Wars. A small evil, serving to prepare the soil for the for the seeds of the greatest evil ever known.

Chapter 1

Europe, in 1939 was a place rife with conflict. Of course, there were the larger conflicts between countries, but some conflicts were even more personal. The people were caught in the throes of a world-wide depression, and tension abounded nearly everywhere. When there is not enough food for one's family, and even more importantly, when there are no means to procure such food, conflict becomes inevitable.

Whether it is the inherent jealousy between those who have sufficient food and shelter and those who do not, or the lack of perceived opportunity, these jealousies can generate their own problems. But there is also the human need to place blame, for blame is the balm that strangely eases the sores of need.

My father, who worked for the United States Government at that time, was fairly lucky. We lived a moderately comfortable life in the city of Baranowo. There were five in my family: my mother and father, little brother Andrew who was only a few weeks old, and my sister Irene. Irene was my best friend and I missed her sorely. She had gone to live with my aunt because my aunt had no children of her own, and she felt badly about this. My mother, to ease her sister's pain, offered to let Irene stay with her. Our house was sufficient for our needs, but the storms that assailed the world, from its leaders to the least among us, would not spare our small lives. It was a typical house of that region. Although we were on the outskirts of town, we had a small plot of land where we grew vegetables. We also had a barn where we kept a cow, a couple of goats, and some geese.

The radio in the living room crackled with static. I sat near my father, looked at the lighted round dial, and listened to the broadcast. It did not seem very important to me, as I was only seven years old. But the grave expression on my father's face was palpable, and the tension I felt in the room was real. The announcer, in tones touched with gravity, said that Germany had just attacked Poland. "I don't like this. Perhaps, we should go to the United States," my father said aloud, but I knew his words were not for me. Instead, they were aimed directly at my mother.

I saw her face cloud over and she turned away. From my adult perspective, I understand why she did this. To her, war was unimportant. She was concerned with her family and our life together. War, while an inconvenience, should not have an effect on one simple family trying to live their lives as best they can.

"I don't know—" she said. My father looked at her and smiled sympathetically. He knew she was thinking of her sisters and parents, who did not have that option.

"Well, if we cannot go to the United States, I think we should get out of the city."

"Where will we go?" My mother asked, emotion choking her voice.

"Let's go stay with your brother in Grabownica."

"I suppose we could. They might like the company, and that certainly is far from the paths of war. Let me write him and ask."

Shortly after this, we loaded our possessions into a wagon and began the move to Grabownica. Our moving was not unusual at this time, as many people were moving out of the cities. Wars centered around the cities, not on the simple folks living deep in the country. I remember helping carry our possessions to the wagon where my father stacked them. I looked at the street where I grew up and the house I lived in and felt sad. Leaving so much of my world behind was hard.

"What about Irene?" I asked.

"She is safe. We'll let her know where we are so she can join us, if necessary." My mother's voice cracked with emotion. I could tell she did not want to leave her friends and church behind. But with two young boys, seeking a place of refuge from the coming war seemed a good idea.

The roads were crowded with individuals and families moving from one place to another to escape the gathering storm. Now, I know we call such people refugees. But when you are seven, such words are beyond your ken. Instead, you perceive that you are moving, and others are moving as well—so nothing seemed amiss.

When we arrived at Grabownica, I was happy. The town was a town in name only. In reality, it was nothing more than a cluster of five houses deep in the midst of a large pine forest. There was a stream that served as the focal point of the settlement. The stream, through countless years, had carved a valley. In this place, all manner of fruit trees abounded, and wild berries and mushrooms grew everywhere. My memories of first seeing this place are wonderful. To me, the land looked like something out of a landscape painting I had seen in a museum.

My father told me that, because it was so far away from the cities, the people here pretty much took care of themselves. They kept livestock and farmed the rich soil. My father also explained that the option of returning to the United States was gone. The Germans were already bombing the cities; it was no longer safe to try to make it to the American Embassy in Warsaw.

When we arrived, we were warmly welcomed. I was glad to see my cousins, who were about the same age. Having someone to occupy the lonely space left by my sister's absence was important, and we got along famously.

The work was hard, but honest. In the evening, after the day's work had been completed and supper finished, the people in the small community would gather and visit. And while telling stories and singing songs used to be the normal activities, of late, the talk had turned to war. And though we were far from the cities where the war was engaged and real, we could not pretend it was beyond our reach.

It had been reported that the Germans were now moving nearer to our small town. We heard they were only forty kilometers away. This seemed a good distance to me, but with a mechanized army, it was not much more than a few hours' journey. The tension the men felt was clear. After listening to the talk one evening, my father asked my uncle, "Where do you think we could build a bomb shelter?"

"You think they will bomb here, Joseph?"

"No, I don't think so. But they may move through the area and I want a place to go where I know my family will be safe. Besides, the Russians are moving in from the East. With the Germans moving in from the West, we are caught in the middle. I think it would be better to have a place where we can go for safe protection.

Again, from an adult perspective, I understand why my father wanted to complete this task. In a village this small, there was little for him to do. He wanted to feel useful and important. And though my father was helping with the farming, it was apparent to him that his help was not necessary. He wanted to do something that would be of use, a project that would give him a sense of contributing to the welfare of all.

The next morning, my uncle took my dad to a place deep in the forest. I went along. "What do you think of this, Joseph?"

"I don't know. I would prefer it to be further from the

road. Let's look a little beyond here."

The three of us walked in the stillness of the deep woods until my father found a place more to his liking. It was similar to the first site, but there were more young trees, which could be used as camouflage for the structure.

It took my dad approximately three days to dig the hole for the shelter. He worked at it from sunup to sundown until he had hollowed out a space large enough for us to hide.

Taking care to move further away from the structure, he cut down tree after tree and made them into logs that would fit closely together to protect us. Dragging these logs through the dense forest was not easy; it took my father another three days to build the four walls and roof. When the structure was completed, he covered it over with some of the dirt he had removed.

As with the completion of any project, there is a sense of satisfaction. We led the rest of the families to the structure and they were impressed. As we made the journey home, we could hear planes flying. Shortly after we heard their roar, the distant thunder of bombs falling on the nearby city of Ostroleka disturbed the silence of the night.

Chapter 2

The planes continued their assault throughout the night. I tried to sleep, but it was difficult with the distant percussion of the bombs invading your consciousness. But the night did pass eventually. However, in the morning the bombers were so thick in the sky that they darkened the sun. The bombing was continuous and lasted for days. This heightened our fear considerably.

My parents were beginning to worry that the communication between my mother and her sister concerning Irene might not have been complete, given the disruptions of the war. And now, there was no way to reach her. "Helen, we cannot stay here forever."

"I know. I'm so worried about home. What if my sister brought Irene back and we weren't there?"

"Do you want to go home?" My father asked with concern audible in his voice.

"Yes, I think it would be best."

I could see that they both were very worried; my mom was crying. I was scared, but I hoped that maybe I would get to see my sister again and we would be together. We moved back to Baranowo.

When we returned home, I was amazed at how many of our friends and relatives were still here. I had expected that more people would be gone. Visiting my grandparents again was wonderful. They told us that there had been German planes bombing in the area. Many people had been killed.

And though most of the city had been spared, there was stark evidence of destruction. The church, which used to have two steeples, now had only one and part of another. Fires the bombing burned everywhere; some of the houses were still smoldering from the previous attack. Everywhere we looked, men were throwing buckets of water on the fire. The fire department was obviously overmatched. It was up to the people themselves to make certain that the structures did not burn to the ground.

As we passed a group of people milling around, we were aware that more and more people were leaving now. If leaving had not seemed a good idea before, the reality of the bombs falling had taught them a different lesson altogether. We also heard that a group of soldiers from the Polish army was hiding in the woods, preparing to surprise the Germans.

That afternoon, in September of 1939, a group of three German motorcycles came out of the woods, just down the road and stopped in front of our house. My father and I were standing outside visiting with our neighbors. The men approached us with their guns in a ready position. I was frightened.

One of the soldiers, wearing sunglasses, spoke. We could not understand him. We did not speak German, and it was obvious that he did not speak Polish. My father reached down and took my small hand in his. It was a comfort to have his strong hand encompass mine. I looked at the soldier and moved closer to my father.

When the soldier spoke, my father tightened his grip. I could feel the rough callouses on his hands, damp with sweat, and I knew he was nervous in a way I'd never felt.

A second German exited from the sidecar of one of the motorcycles and asked us questions in German. We shook our heads, indicating we did not understand. He took his rifle and began pointing it, not directly at us, but in a menacing manner.

Another soldier had drawn a hand-held machine gun and was pointing it at us with the most ghastly smile I had ever seen. They kept repeating the question, first to my father, and then to the neighbors. All shook their heads, "No."

Finally, they assumed there was nothing to be learned, and they moved on. Later, my dad told me they wanted to know if there was a Polish army in the forest nearby.

But the soldiers on the motorcycle were not the only ones on the road that day. In the distance, we could hear the rumble of tanks, half-tracks, and mechanized artillery coming closer, disturbing the silence of an otherwise quiet afternoon.

All that day the procession continued moving toward the train station at Jastrzabka. At dusk the procession stopped. As the day ended, we could see the sun resting peacefully against the horizon—as though it was a painting disconnected from the palpable fear in our village.

Just before full dark, the gunfire erupted. My father grabbed me and yelled, "Get down! Crawl into the unfinished rooms!"

I had little choice, I did as I was told. My father hovered over to protect me. My mother picked up Andrew, and we watched as she moved ahead of us. We moved as quickly as we could. When I felt the sand in my hands, there was some sense of relief. It represented, at least temporarily, a haven.

I had never been so frightened in my life. Bullets were hitting the house and causing a tremendous clatter. We huddled together in the rooms that had white sand for floors with a sturdy foundation. My mother was praying aloud, my father was quiet.

The battle raged for nearly an hour. We could hear countless bullets fly overhead, as if they were angry hornets. Some of them chinked off the foundation and more than a few perforated the house. Then, silence. A pervasive silence that beckoned all to be still.

But that was not to be. In a very short time, the noise of a plane flying overhead broke the silence and we were pulled back to that unreal reality once again. My father took advantage of the lull in the fighting to rush into the house and rip the bedding from the beds. He came back as quickly as he could, his arms full of blankets and pillows. My father lovingly put his hand on my mother's shoulder to reassure her. My brother Andrew and I were laying down between them. As Andrew cried, my father let his hand fall onto Andrew's back and rubbed gently. I could feel him lower his arm so that he touched me as well. It felt reassuring. We spent the night huddled in the darkness.

Chapter 3

There are many levels of terror. I know this now. As an old man, I am aware that life has a way of teaching us these lessons whether we are willing students or not. But in my memories, this single night stands out among most others, because I was being made acutely aware of the nature of fear. This fear seeped into me as we huddled together, while the bullets screeched their song of death above and shattered my world.

Baranowo, in the Polish countryside, was not a large town. In reality, at that time it was nothing more than a semi-rural village. Our house, on the outskirts of town, was not a farm, and my father was not a farmer. However, we did keep animals, and we had a barn. We raised the animals to supplement my father's income. This was neither unusual nor unexpected. It was part of everyday life.

The month of September in Baranowo was like the month of September nearly everywhere in the temperate areas of our world. While the days can be warm and inviting, the nights carry the cutting edge of winter in their restless breezes—a bittersweet time that both beckons and repels us. The certain knowledge exists that while harvest time is nearly always one of the most delightful times of the year, each passing day brings us closer to winter.

For once, there even seemed enough to eat. The crops were harvested or being harvested, and food was abundant. This was a relief as for the last few months, food was becoming more and more scarce.

The morning after that night of terror dawned gloriously. As the sun kissed the sleeping land awake, I stretched in my blankets and instinctively reached for my parents. I felt a need to touch them, to know absolutely that they were there and safe and ready to protect me. When I could not find them, the terror suppressed through my sleep erupted, and I screamed, "Mom! Dad!"

My father rushed into the room, his face showing love and concern; he picked me up and held me close. I clung to him and nestled my face into his shoulder. Grateful tears dampened my face as he hugged me tightly.

"Mitchell, Mitchell, everything is fine. Your mother and brother are fine. We simply let you sleep. Now, calm down. We are here."

I clung tightly, safe in the security of my father's arms for long moments. Finally, he began moving out of the room toward the main rooms of the house, carrying me in his strong arms. I knew he was bringing me to Mom, and that knowledge warmed me with a rush.

My mother welcomed me with open arms, and I left my father and clung to her tightly. I held her close and never wanted to release her. We listened, in the quiet of that morning, to hear if last night's fighting was continuing. Instead of the sound of guns and machinery, we heard nothing but an overwhelming silence. Pervasive and complete, it shuttered the day with an incredible stillness. But life has to move on, and she soon hugged me tightly and said, "Mitchell, I have work to do. Now, go to your father."

My father was staring out of the window, and I walked quickly to his side, took his hand in mine, and joined my gaze with his. I looked toward the blacksmith shop at the far end of town and viewed a sight I will never forget. There was an imposing pine forest at that end of town. Hanging from the lower branches of the mighty pines, were four German soldiers.

My father, noticing where I was looking, took me in his

arms once again and said, "Don't look."

There was not much wind that day, for it seemed as if the world itself were taking a respite from the fighting. But what little breeze there was caused the hanging bodies to move mysteriously. They drew my eyes and locked their focus on what would have been unthinkable a few days before.

When I saw the German soldiers hanging, I felt confused and weak. While I had been instructed that the Germans were our enemies, it was not in my heart to have enough hatred to wish them killed and disrespected.

My father, noticing my anxiety, took my hand and gently pulled me away from the window. I had a million questions to ask. I looked my father in the eye and asked, "Dad, why are these soldiers carrying these guns and coming here?"

There it was, a simple question without a simple answer.

My father was taken aback but felt the need to respond. He hugged me again and said, "Because the Germans are invading Poland."

"But why?"

"I don't know. I guess it is because they are the Germans."

This seemed to be too much of a non-answer, so I persisted, "Why? What do we have that they want?"

"I simply do not know, Mitchell."

At this moment, the foreign fear I'd experienced the night before was recast like clay into an unrefutable knowledge that our happiness, our very way of living, had been changed. We had been changed—forever. With an awful weight, we had been secured in a dark insecurity. All that remained was terror and a feeling of helplessness.

Chapter 4

The clouds of memory have a way of making us see what we would like to see, instead of what actually happened. It is inevitable and very human. But with all of my experiences, I clearly remember my father and mother as being good Christian people who were always willing to help those less fortunate—even if they did not share the same beliefs. I believe that is simply how they were, and when I think about them, I know they were this way.

The capture of my city by the Germans led to many changes. Jewish people were being arrested and imprisoned in a hastily-constructed facility on the edge of town. While it was primarily the Jews being arrested, it certainly was not entirely Jews. Quite a few ordinary Polish citizens were also kept in these camps, people who were suspected of helping the Jews or men who might serve as a threat to the German army.

At my house, the last few days had been filled with endless discussions about what to do. My mother wanted to leave Baranowo to go back to Grabownica and stay with her brother. My father did not think it necessary, as he was an American citizen. He had been born in the United States, and at this time, the United States had not entered the war. "I really do not think we have to be overly concerned. I am an American; I cannot believe the Germans would want to bother us. Besides, what are we going to do if Irene comes back and we are not here?"

With pain hanging like a veil over her face, my mother, said, "I know. But you speak of reason in these times? What reason demands they arrest normal people? What reason forces these people into prisons, when they have done nothing wrong?"

"I know. You're correct, but listen—the battle has already passed us here. I expect that nothing bad will happen."

Even as he spoke these words, we could hear the percussion of the big German guns as they attacked the city of Ostroleka on their way to Warsaw.

After we finished supper, we went to the barn to check on the animals for the evening. This was a necessary nightly chore to ensure they had sufficient water and fresh hay. As we left the house, we looked on a world of darkness. Even though we were in the city and there should have been light, there was none. The Germans had said, in the rules of occupation that had been posted in the town square, that anyone using a light would be killed. Having seen the brutality of the Germans, we would not break their rule. However, the uncommon darkness was pervasive, and we stumbled several times over rough patches on our way to the barn.

My father slowly opened the door to the barn and tried to peer into the darkness. When we had experienced as much as we had, my father was reluctant to take chances. Ahead of us, in the deeper shadows, we caught a movement. My father quickly pushed me behind him. "Who's there?" he asked, his voice trembling.

"Joseph, it is Moshe."

Moshe was my father's long-time friend, and they greeted each other with a strong hug. "Joseph, the Germans..."

"I know. They are arresting your people. What can I do?"

"I don't know.... Do you know of a place where we could stay—away from all of this?" His breathing was short and shallow between the words.

"There is a room under the floor of the barn. I was going to finish it into a cellar, but I ran out of money to purchase cement and..."

"I know, the war. Do you think it's safe?"

"I'm not sure. I know that we can cover the door so it can escape detection, but beyond that I cannot say."

My father retrieved a pitchfork and pulled the hay away to expose a door in the floor. Together, Moshe and my father opened the door and ushered Moshe's wife Ursula and two children, Shlamo their son, and Rivka their daughter, into the room. They, too, must have been hovering in our barn's darkness. Once they were situated, my father and Moshe moved the few possessions they had managed to bring with them into the unfinished cellar.

"There are more families, Joseph. You have any idea of where they might go?"

"Let me think a moment. When we went to Grabownica, I built a bunker in the woods. As far as I know, no one is using it. Do you think they might like to try it?"

"Perhaps. How will they live?"

"I am certain that our relatives will care for them. Grabownica is a small place with good people. It is far from anything that the Germans might find desirable. I think your friends would be safe there. How many are there?"

"Three or four families. I hate to ask this, as you have done so much already, but do you think you could take them there?"

"I am pretty sure I can."

Having done what we could to get them settled and comfortable, we headed back to the house. My father told my mother about Moshe and his family. Her face showed great concern, but she knew this was the right thing to do. My father turned to us and said, "Listen, you are not to mention this to anyone. I'm not sure what the Germans would do if they found out, but I do not want to know either." He looked at each of us, and we agreed.

With measured words he continued: "Now, I need to take these families that Moshe told me are waiting in the forest to Grabownica. This has to be done under cover of darkness and immediately." I followed him as he approached the door. He looked at me as if he wanted to say he couldn't take me with him. After hesitating a moment, he quietly motioned for me to come.

When we reached the forest, my dad told them about the bunker and our relatives in that city. They agreed to make the journey We accompanied four Jewish families with several children to Grabownica that night. When we arrived and after introductions, Father told my aunt and uncle to take good care of the families. I was sure they would. We heard later that one of the Jewish men joined the Polish Underground Fighters' Resistance.

In the months that followed, I seldom saw any evidence of Moshe and his family living in the barn. My mother would share what little food we had with them. But during a war the first casualty is food. There is less of it, and what little there is lacks in quality. So, ordinary people suffer more. War simply makes it too hard to do the things necessary to either earn a living or to cultivate the land to produce food.

While the harvest had been a good one, the occupying German army had confiscated all but a pittance. There simply was precious little to eat. I became ill from the lack of food. I became thin and wan and longed for the most simple of all pleasures: enough to eat. My hunger was so complete that I did not even have much preference as to what my dream feast would be. To tell the truth, anything would have been wonderful.

Sometimes, I would lie awake at night because I couldn't sleep—the pain of hunger can rob even this simple pleasure.

There was so much happening in my world that it was confusing. I did not understand why people were being arrested and mistreated. It did not make sense to me. Since I could not sleep, I dwelled on these events. I also thought about how hungry I was. This knowledge of the nature of hunger was a new one to me. Before the war, I thought I knew what hunger was. I was wrong. The hunger we feel when have not eaten for a few hours or a day is much different than this.

This hunger was so pervasive that it makes thinking of anything else difficult. But as badly as we had it, Moshe's family had it worse. At least we were free to move about in the sunshine and visit with our friends. In the room below our barn, I knew that Moshe's family was living a life of extreme isolation, and that was a bad thing.

During the ten months that Moshe and his family stayed, we often would go foraging for food together. Although, there was not very much food around; and if you could find it, it was very expensive. We often had to steal in order to eat.

Is it so wrong, in God's eyes, to steal? It is a question I have reflected on my entire life. I have never reached a satisfying answer. Yes, stealing is a wrong. The Ten Commandments state it clearly: *Thou shalt not steal*. But isn't surviving to serve the Lord a good thing? So, a conundrum occurs. It has no answer, but I can speak from experience that if you are faced with stealing or starving, the choice is an easy one.

The animals we had kept were now gone. Hunger and need had driven us to butcher them. It is hard to plan for the future when you are so hungry that it seems as though there is no time beyond the present. Besides, if we had not butchered them, the Germans would have. They were confiscating everything that was worthwhile in the town of Baranowo, including the livestock.

Often, Moshe, my father, and I would sneak into the darkness in search of food. We carried simple burlap sacks over our shoulders, and we hoped to come back with a couple of chickens or some potatoes.

I think they brought me along because, as a young boy, I was more agile than they were. I was also smaller and could sneak into places more easily. This gave me a feeling of contributing, and I liked it. It was a good experience to be given an adult's responsibility before I had yet reached the age of eight.

What did we steal? Nearly anything we could to survive—chickens, potatoes, and other vegetables, and occasionally a piglet. But we had to be very careful with these, because they tended to squeal too loudly, and this could lead to discovery.

Stealing in a war zone is a crime punishable, as most crimes were, by death. If we had been caught, there was little doubt that our bodies would be the ones hanging at the far end of town by the blacksmith's shop.

I will always remember walking alongside the road, not on it, by the light of the moon, taking care to keep our footsteps as quiet as possible so not to be discovered. Dogs are the worst enemy of those who are trying to practice stealth. Luckily, there were only a few dogs left in the area. When there is not enough food for the humans to eat, it seemed silly to try to keep a companion animal. Besides, under the rule of occupation: Polish people were not permitted to keep dogs. I never asked where the dogs had gone; I guess I did not want to know the answer.

My father took the families to Grabownica and left them there. They remained safe throughout the war. In times of crisis, the best of us often comes to the forefront. My parents and their people were good people.

Chapter 5

One night, we robbed old man Robakowski of his chickens. The sky was moonless. The late fall is not a pleasant time to be out. There was a chill in the air and a feeling that it could either rain or snow at any moment. With as much stealth as my small body could muster, I followed the two men into the barnyard. Father and Moshe held the fence apart for me to slip through. I crawled toward the chicken house as quietly as I could. I did not want to raise any alarm with the birds or any other animals. I saw the small house as a ghostly apparition before me. When I had managed to cross to the shed without detection, I felt the rough-hewn boards with my hand as I raised myself to a standing position. With my hands barely moving, I fingered the latch until it clicked open. Searching the darkness to make certain there was no one alerted to our presence, I opened the door. It creaked softly. Although I didn't think that the sound was loud enough to raise the alarm, I did hear the chickens begin chattering.

Readying my bag, I moved into the chicken house and reached for two of the largest chickens I could see in the half-light. I took one and stuffed it in the bag while I tried to hold the other between my knees. It fought gallantly, and I had to squeeze my legs together with a great deal of force to hold it captive.

The birds had now sounded the alarm, and I quickly stuffed the other chicken in the bag and ran toward my father and Moshe. They held the fence open for me, and we ran down the side of the road toward home.

My father took the bag containing the chickens and felt

around until he could identify their necks; he then twisted their heads violently. They were still. I don't believe he thought very much about this. It was simply a fact of living in the country. The chickens meant little to him, and it was necessary that they not sound the alarm. Later, I equated this with how the Germans treated us. A cold indifference is the best way I can explain it. But the chickens tasted good when we ate them the next day. We saved the bones to make soup, and it lasted that entire week.

There were other things we did to survive as well. One of the best ways I discovered was to steal from the Germans. When the German army traveled through town, they would park their vehicles in the middle of our town square area in a circle. The soldiers would rest and find shelter away from the trucks.

I would wait until everyone was distracted or busy performing some other duty, sneak up to the wagons, and see what was available to steal. Often, I managed to get bread. Other times blankets and anything else that was there. Although they bore the hated swastika, the blankets were put to good use by my mother. She would remove the symbol and dye the blankets.

She then used the material to make coats and blankets and even pants. The material was a godsend for us. We had no money to purchase ready-made clothes or even material to make new ones. It is hard for us to imagine, in this time when everything is so plentiful, that there were times when it was not.

Late one evening, when I was returning home from raiding the Germans, I saw two Gendarmes, German police, coming down the street toward me. At that very moment, the clouds parted, and the full light of the moon shone on the bright snow. I was clearly visible, carrying my stolen goods.

I did not know what to do. With my arms full, I ran for an opening under a neighbor's porch. I tried my best not to make any noise. When I ran from the road, I tried my best to follow the footprints that were already present in the snow. But the last few feet by the opening to the porch were covered by a pristine blanket of white.

The Gendarmes were coming closer, and their dogs, Alsatians, were staring at me as I huddled in the damp darkness. I had placed my loot, a couple of loaves of bread and a blanket, under me to try to keep them from view.

The dogs, ever restless, stared at me—looking deeply into my eyes. I prayed as hard as I ever have that the dogs would not voice their discovery. "Oh, God, please help me," I implored silently. One of the dog's lips curled, and I waited for either the growl or bark that would make their masters aware of my presence. For whatever reason, the dogs did not bark. When they had passed, I ran from my hiding place for home. It was not very far, perhaps only three hundred feet, but it seemed as though it were the other side of the world. When I entered the door, I felt a relief I had never experienced. That had been so close. I know that the Germans would have killed me for stealing. I was fortunate; I thanked the Lord for helping me one more time.

That fall soon turned into winter. I am not certain that the winters then were that much more severe than they are now. But because of our situation of not having enough to eat or even proper clothing to wear, they certainly seemed that way.

When things became really difficult, I would go to where the Germans placed their garbage and root through it like a hog searching for something edible. A piece of old bread or a half-eaten piece of meat was welcomed. I think of it now, and it disgusts me. But the choice between eating garbage and surviving was an easy one. The Germans were so demanding that even this simple, and dehumanizing, activity had to be done under cover of darkness and with great stealth.

I have thought about their mendacity often and have come to the conclusion that they simply cared little whether we lived or died. Our survival was not any of their concern. Their only concern was their ultimate victory, and anything that stood in the way of this was considered to be a simple obstacle to be overcome or dominated.

As the sole arbiters of goodness and justice, they believed that their goals were paramount. Whether we survived, had enough to eat, or a place to sleep out of the cold was truly irrelevant to them.

At this time, my mother was becoming more and more concerned about my sister Irene. We had not heard from her in several months, and our experiences with the German occupation were not easing our minds on this part. We had witnessed their brutality many times, and our fear for Irene was real. We had tried sending a letter, but the postal service was not functioning properly. There were no telephones for the people to use, and our only hope was in sending a message by someone going to that area. So far, this had proved unsuccessful.

My mother would often sit at the kitchen table, stare past the barn into the deep woods, and cry. We did our best to comfort her, but in the end, what could we say? We hoped that she was doing well. We believed that she was, but we did not know. There is a difference between believing something and knowing something. Beliefs are colored by experiences, and knowledge is sure and true.

Traveling in a war zone is difficult. My grandfather told us that he would go east and try to find a way through Russia to the south and reenter Poland. My father felt as though he wanted to go with him, but this knowledge was tempered by the fact that he also had an obligation to stay and protect us.

During this time, our fear of the Germans was increasing. Every passing day brought some new atrocity to our attention. We realized how precarious our situation was, with my family sheltering Moshe's. We decided that we should try to finish the cellar and make an escape tunnel into the woods.

Before it got really cold, my dad, Moshe, and I finished the cellar and a small tunnel leading from the cellar into the wooded area just in case someday Moshe and his family had to escape or we had to escape with them.

With time on our hands, it gave us a feeling of accomplishment to do this. Besides, we could not be caught in this situation. Instant death was soon to follow. In the last few months I had seen so much death that I was acutely aware of how closely it lurked—just waiting for me to make a mistake.

We carried the dirt out of the cellar in buckets and walked into the woods and spread it out so that it would not be obvious that there was a tunnel. That task was pretty much left to me. My father and Moshe worked on the tunnel, and I carried the dirt into the woods.

The tunnel took a long time to complete, but what else had we to do? We had worked the sectors of land we usually did, but after the Germans came and confiscated most of what we had grown, there simply was not enough to eat. In truth, there was not even enough to survive after the Germans took most of the potatoes and wheat—that is, without stealing.

Chapter 6

I have always been told that time is a constant and that it does not change as we go from day to day. But in my experience, this is not true. Simply, there are periods when we feel that time is slowed until it seems we are standing still. Made captive by something that is so significant, our perceptions are attenuated. We see not only what is happening at that particular moment, but things that have already happened, and sometimes, under very special circumstances, a future.

Is this portrayal of the future accurate? I don't know. I have experienced many of these time anomalies in my seven decades, and I cannot state unequivocally that they show with any certainty the future. But I am not one who will claim that their veracity is suspect. Perhaps, as we move through our lives, there are choices and events that affect these possible futures. All I know is that when we experience one of these times of heightened consciousness, the forces afoot can have a devastating effect on our lives, and even on history.

The months continued to pass us by, and still there was no word of Irene. My mother was becoming increasingly agitated. She would often sit and cry at the window. Her sleep was troubled, and she became more and more listless.

My father had harbored some hope that his father would send word about Irene. But as the days crept into weeks and months with no word, our hopes faded. Finally, my father, in order to calm both my mom and himself, decided to risk the journey to see if he could find her.

On a nearly cloudless, cold winter morning, he packed an

old satchel with extra clothing and whatever food the family could spare and went to the train station in Jastrzabkeoabke. My father did not want to take me along. It was dangerous, and he knew it. But I ran ahead and waited for him on the road. Reluctantly, he took me with him. I suppose he relented because I was becoming more and more useful as a thief, a small person whom others did not readily notice. Besides, he felt that a man and his son raised much less suspicion than a solitary man traveling.

We walked to the train station through the bleak landscape. On the rise of a hill just above the station, we saw something that is burned, as if by a branding iron, forever in my memory. At first what lay before us appeared no more than a bleak watercolor painting. As we gazed, it seemed that everyone and everything was locked into their positions, as if they were afraid to move. It is a scene I will never forget.

As we stared at the gauzy images, we tried to understand what we were seeing. Our vision was disturbed by an approaching train as its mournful whistle ripped the sky. Its stack belched dark clouds into the still blue and white world, and its driving wheels beat out a mechanical background.

Nazis were lining the tracks. Spaced about thirty feet apart, they stood with their weapons ready. Some carried rifles, and a few had automatic weapons, but all were poised for action.

As the train entered the station, we could see that the train's cars, usually reserved for transporting livestock, were filled with people. Even with a casual glance, I could see that these people looked no more than walking skeletons. They were so pale and thin, bones were clearly visible in their hands and faces as they pressed against the slats, exposing them to the elements. I thought they looked like they were already dead, and I wanted to avert my eyes. I did not. Instead, some force drew me to stare at this maudlin scene.

As the train came to a stop, I noticed that a board on the side of one of the cars had come loose. A young Jewish woman delicately pushed a small infant through the crack. Why she did this, I have never understood. What did she hope to accomplish? To this day I cannot say that I know with any certainty. I suppose if I had been her, I might have done the same. But of this, I am less than sure. I understand it better now, but I still do not think I could have done what she did.

A German soldier moved toward the baby where it lay crying on the white snow. I reached for my father and felt his strong arm on my shoulder as he pulled me close. The soldier stood over the baby with his weapon in a firing position. It looked as if he were readying the gun for firing, but my mind would not let me believe that anyone could do this. The mother managed to jump from the car but landed wrong. When she tried to walk, it was obvious that her leg was broken. Disregarding the pain, she began moving toward the baby, hopping on her good leg and dragging the other behind her. From my vantage point, I could see the panic and hatred in her eyes. The soldier's upper lip twitched as he walked close to the infant, lowered his rifle to the baby's head, looked the other way, and squeezed the trigger.

The mother's scream ripped from her heart as she limped pitifully toward the soldier. As the seconds passed, I could tell she was cursing him as strongly as I have ever heard anyone curse another. As I stared, I realized that she looked like she was on the verge of death as she staggered to her dead baby.

Helplessly, with tears streaming, she told the soldier that his time was coming. With no expression whatsoever, the soldier raised his weapon to her head and pulled the trigger again and again.

With each retort of the rifle, an involuntary spasm rocked my body. These visions are still with me. I cannot erase them from my consciousness. They have become part of me, and damn them for that. In that moment I learned that hate is not always a bad word. Sometimes, hate is necessary to understand that which cannot be understood without the benefit of this lens to sharpen our focus.

I heard my father cry, "Oh, my God!" I looked at him. His face was pale, and he clenched his fists time and again. I turned my head toward him, clung closely, and let my tears fall.

Chapter 7

With this terrible scene burned irrevocably into our eyes, we realized that we would not be able to board the train at this station. It had been our plan to simply hop on one of the boxcars and ride as close as we could get to where my sister might be. But with the soldiers lining the tracks here, this idea had to be discarded. "Mitch, we had better leave and go to the next station." I agreed, and we skirted the station and the scene of horror and headed down the tracks again.

While we were not doing anything that could be considered wrong, we certainly did not want to chance dealing with men like we had just seen.

"Mitchell, the trains just slow at the next station. They do not stop. We'll have to jump. Can you do it?"

"I think so," I answered. In truth, I was not so much worried about me as I was my father. I was a young boy and jumping was natural for me. But I thought we could make it.

As I walked through the desolation of winter, my mind could not leave the scene I had just witnessed. Walking in the cold, my mind racing, was disconcerting. Finally, I stopped and turning to my father, I asked, "Dad, I don't understand. Why did she throw the baby out of the car?"

Furrows in my father's face were filled with pain. I could tell the question was one that he had been contemplating as well. He looked at the ground in front of us, shrugged his shoulders imperceptibly, and said, "I honestly don't know. I can guess that perhaps they were starving, and she was looking for some compassion from the Nazis. But I don't know. I guess we will never know. It is impossible to understand."

Seeing that this question could have no answer and the incident was too close to us, I dropped the subject and walked quietly, holding my father's hand. That seemed to be the only grasp of comfort within my reach—and perhaps my father's.

We found the next station; luckily, it was nearly deserted. The train's whistle signaled its approach, and we readied ourselves. My father stood behind me to help in case I did not make a clean jump. We were hiding in the brush alongside the track as the train passed. When we saw a nearly deserted car, my father said, "Get ready." I tensed my muscles and bent in a crouch. When the train was near enough, I jumped. My father followed immediately. I felt his strong arm supporting me as we made our way into the nearly deserted car and sat.

The train, my father told me, was bound for Ostroleka and then Wyszkow. We rode in silence, ever fearful of discovery. Those on the train with us did the same. I think of it now, and it seems strange that such deep communication can be mounted without the use of words. There was much to say, but no way to say it. Instead, plaintive eyes and soft sighs were given and then returned. The look in our eyes told of the trials we had already gone through and, more importantly, those that were yet to come. Fatalism is a disease that is infectious, and we shared it, if not willingly, then freely.

When we got near to Ostroleka, we jumped from the train and continued our journey by walking through the woods. This was necessary, my father explained, because we did not want to enter the station without the proper traveling authority. This authority was given in the form of specially designated papers. We did not have these, and as with most activities in a combat zone, traveling without the proper authorization was a crime.

We continued moving through these towns, hopping a

train where we could, walking where there were no trains available or the danger was too high. We finally came to the town of Bialystok in Russia. Crossing the border had not been a problem as we crossed far from any checkpoints or authorities. My father had friends nearby, and he had heard that, perhaps, Irene might have been imprisoned here. But it was in Russia, and they were also at war with my country at that time. It was dangerous, and the tension we felt was real.

Information in a war is always difficult. The truth is, we did not know that Irene was here. We did not even know if my father's friend was here. When we entered the town, just before dark, we did not know what to expect.

My father led us to his friend's house and knocked. I stayed in the shadows and was told, "Mitchell, if anything happens, you must run and get back home the best way you can. Do you understand?"

I nodded that I did, but the truth is that I could not imagine it coming to that. My father was so strong and fearless; I could not conceive of anything happening to him.

The door opened and we heard, "Joseph, what are you doing here? Come in. Come in."

Finding my father's friends was an indescribable relief. They welcomed us into their home and shared their meager food with us. It felt good to sleep in a place with a roof over my head after sleeping in the bleak forest the last few nights.

Traveling in Russia was as risky as traveling in Poland. The Russians and Germans had signed a pact agreeing to split Poland. The pact was not based in ideology, but rather in mutual greed. The Germans lusted after Poland, as did the Russians. My father told me as we were walking that last August they had signed what he called a non-aggression treaty. I did not really understand and probed more. My father explained it in more detail, but I still did not understand. It seemed so wrong. We had done nothing to them; why were they at war with us? My father had no answers, but the question lingered.

My father's friend, who seemed to be a man with some connections, managed to find out that although Irene was not being held here, my grandfather and my Aunt Sophie were. He paid off the guards so that we could go and visit them.

Walking into the prison at Bialystok was another stark lesson in the cruelty of one human being to another. I had never experienced such filth! We perceive our world by using our senses. Most people, by now, have seen pictures depicting the people's conditions in the war. The problem with these photographs is that they cannot communicate the depth of squalor, degradation, and humiliation. The smell of that area is one that is with me to this day. There were no sanitary facilities whatsoever. The stench of urine and feces permeated the air to the extent that when one breathed, it was sickening.

The faces of those arrested and in prison will never leave me either. All humans have some form of hope shining in their eyes. But not here. All left of these people were empty shells, recognizable by their human form. But, somehow they had been pushed beyond caring and planning for the future and into a docile acceptance of their fates. Moaning, instead of talking, seemed to be the means of communication.

Rats abounded everywhere. Apparently, the prisoners were either too feeble to bother with them or indifferent to their presence. Perhaps, they had fought a losing battle and now accepted these parasitic creatures as fellow prisoners. Either way, the rats were bold and cocky, as though they had claimed squatters' rights, even over these poor people.

I moved closer to my father as we moved deeper into the prison. I tried to hide my face in his coat to alleviate the smell and to feel his strength as we moved our way past hundreds of lost souls. Finally, we rounded a corner, and the guard took a set of keys from his belt and fitted one into the lock. We looked inside.

When we saw our relatives, we started to let out a happy noise. The guard turned toward us with a sharp grimace. Though he said nothing, the implication was clear: Be still. My father rushed ahead and hugged his sister tightly and then repeated this to my grandfather. My grandfather did not look well. He was nearly blind, my aunt told us, from the lice eating into his eyes. His eyes were dead—lifeless, expressionless. He was unshaven, with a long beard, and leaning against the wall. My aunt walked to my father and pulled him away. My father turned and asked, "What happened, Sophie?"

"We were arrested in Lomza. They accused us of being spies. Of all things! But I am sure it will be straightened out —eventually. But I have been told the Russians plan to move us further into Russia."

"Where?"

"A work camp near Moscow."

"When?"

"I don't know. I am guessing soon. But I don't think Father will make it."

My dad nodded. But the tears formed as he went to his father and hugged him tenderly. I heard him whisper, "I love you, Dad."

Turning to the guard, he asked, "Is there anything we can do to get them released?"

The guard simply shook his head no, and we let it drop. At that moment the guard signaled that we should leave. He told us that the commander was on his way and it had become very dangerous for us to stay any longer. With wistful looks and an utter sense of powerlessness, we said goodbye and walked out of the prison.

The air on the outside had never smelled so sweet before, and I drank of it deeply.

Chapter 8

As we left Bialystok, Irene found her way into my thoughts once again. I missed her gentle companionship. In truth, I did not understand why she had gone to live with my aunt. I knew they were better off than us because they had no children, but I think it was more than that. Childless couples, who love children, need them around. It gives their lives meaning. My mother told me later that she was helping her sister by letting Irene stay there. I guess I understood. But I still missed my sister.

Irene and I were very close. She was nearly my age and had been a constant companion. When she was in the first grade and I was in kindergarten, we used to walk home together from school. I laughed as I remembered that she always wanted to go straight home. I did not. I wanted to play. I used to put my arms around a telephone pole, and she would put her arms around me trying to pull me away so I would go home with her. She was my sister and my best friend, and I loved her. I did not realize how much I loved her until she was gone. I missed her terribly.

As we walked in silence, I closed my eyes occasionally and asked God why everything had to be so complicated. In truth, I wanted my simple life back again—my sister and brother and going to school and doing the things we used to do. But war has a way of changing everything.

We were traveling in the Ukraine, a part of Russia just over the border from Poland. But still Russia. As we walked on that winter's day, I was hoping that my father would want to head for home. I was beginning to miss my mother, brother and home.

"Dad, are we going home now?" I asked.

"I think so. We'll have to travel by the back way, do you understand?"

"Why?" I asked.

"We are traveling without papers. It is necessary that we travel without being found."

The gravity in my father's voice convinced me, and I nodded.

The trip home took us through the deep forest. Occasionally, we found a Polish family who would host us for the evening. At that time, it was customary for people to open their homes to strangers. In part, there was a tradition of hospitality in country towns and villages. In those troubled times, there was another unspoken reason: information that the stranger could provide was a very valuable commodity. When all that you know is filtered through limited government channels, there is a hunger for news. But even in times of war, people are simply people. That is the lesson I was taught that long ago winter's journey home. I know that, after sleeping in the cold, dark wood, the farmhouses with their homey smells and warm beds were most welcome.

Even if we were not invited into the house, we were nearly always welcome to sleep out of the cold in the barn, a most pleasant alternative to nothing at all. On our way, we stopped in the city of Ostroleka. There, we saw the sky filled with German planes. The sound deafened us as we walked. It seemed there were hundreds of them flying just overhead. I could see the black crosses etched on their wings against the cold gray skies.

In a shallow breath my father said, "Some people from town said that they were on their way to bomb Warsaw." As it turns out, they were correct; the German bombing annihilated the city of Warsaw. When their bombers were finished, hardly a brick touched another through mortar. The devastation was nearly complete.

While we were in Ostroleka, we stopped at my cousin's house. My father's sister lived here. We were greeted and stayed with them several days. I remember how excited I was because they had a boy just about my age. Jurek was six months older, and we liked the same things. Even in time of war, children will be children. After we got used to each other, we had a good time.

We would have stayed longer, but my father heard from another friend that his sister's husband might be a German collaborator. We did not stay long after that suspicion was raised. Instead we headed back to the woods for the journey home. Our position was too dangerous to chance it.

From Ostroleka we traveled through the forests again. While we were walking, we would occasionally meet small groups of the Polish army. They would approach us with mistrust, but seeing we were unarmed allayed their fears, and they soon lowered their weapons.

The Polish army had been scattered from their units by the Germans and were mounting whatever resistance they could: ambushes by night, frontal attacks on their barracks under the cover of darkness, and an occasional foray into a daylight skirmish. It was a daunting task, but they did the best they could, even though the helplessness in their eyes revealed a real understanding that there was little they could do.

While we walked most of the way, sometimes we were able to hitch a ride with a farmer. This was most appreciated, because our feet were tired and cold from walking. On one of these occasions, a farmer offered us a ride. He was on his way to market with whatever the soldiers had left him, and he welcomed company. As we exchanged information, he told us of several mass graves just outside of the city.

Rounding a corner, he pointed one of them out. "Apparently, they gathered these poor people, and those who were able to work were forced to dig a pit. Then, they methodically machine-gunned them down into the pit. Look at that! They did not even have the decency to cover them completely."

My eyes followed his hand to behold a sight I will never forget. It was another one of those moments when time slowed and I truly saw, not as a casual observer, but rather, as a part of the scene. With the vision of the soldier murdering the young woman and her baby still seering my consciousness, this was more than I could take. I averted my eyes and wept into my father's coat. His hand caressed the back of my head and pressed me gently against him.

Even with my eyes forced into darkness, I could not shake the grim, lifeless profiles that had commanded my line of vision a moment before. Men, women, and even tiny children were piled randomly on top of each other. And although it was cold, the bodies were decomposing, and the fetid smell assaulted my senses. Tears burst from deep within me, and my father bent and hugged me tightly.

Words were not spoken among us; what words could be said? But the darkness of evil was obliterating the light of our being. We simply did not know what to think. We all have a matrix of comprehension that guides us in our lives. This did not fit into anything we had learned to expect. Even my father was taken aback by the scene and shed bitter tears.

When a man cries, it is usually an indication that something has affected him deeply. This was certainly reason enough. Every one of these people deserved a better fate than this. Though I tried to avoid seeing them, as the soldiers shot one after another for refusing to dig, I realized the desperation they must have felt. I could tell my father did as well. His tears confirmed that dreadful bond. For an instant, it seemed we were not father and son, but brothers witnessing evil.

There was nothing we could do. We moved on. The three

of us mounted the wagon without a word. The silence of deep offense is not easily disturbed. But the farmer had to turn away from this road; when we reached a junction, he said, "I have to head back this way now, I wish I could take you further."

"Thank you for the ride," my father said as he hopped down and held his arms for me. I stepped off the wagon and followed him. The farmer waved goodbye, and we returned the gesture for a long moment. What we had witnessed together left us more than strangers.

We were getting closer and closer to Baranowo. My father said that we were only about seven kilometers from home now. I began to get excited. It had been a long time now since I had been home. It has been my experience that the thought of home can ease the pain of traveling and lighten your footsteps. The knowledge that we would be home within a couple of hours made us dare to feel a spark of joy even in the midst of this chaos.

We walked in silence. When we got to the bridge that led to Baranowo, we noticed that there were German soldiers everywhere. My father saw this and said, "We will have to cross upstream a ways."

We walked parallel to the river until we rounded a wooded bend. My father picked me up on his shoulders and waded across. I know the river was deathly cold, but it was not a large river, and my father walked quickly. And the knowledge that home was on the other side was enough to keep him going.

I could tell my father was cold, but as one landmark after another came into sight, we walked more quickly. Arriving home late in the afternoon was a joyous feeling, one of my happiest that year. Mother embraced us both and welcomed us inside where it was warm. My mom was disappointed that we had no word of Irene, but she was glad to see us. Painfully, Dad started to tell her about our journey and our experiences.

Chapter 9

So many things had happened, and we had seen so much, that the telling took a long time. As my father told of the young woman's desperation, my mother's eyes welled with tears. When we told of the mass grave we had seen, they fell. "Oh, Joseph. What are we to do?" She whispered through the tears.

"The best we can, I guess." He said this as she clung to him tightly and let the tears fall on his strong chest.

For long moments he held her. I watched as his own eyes glistened. He circled her body and drew her closer, lending his strength in this time of need. Finally, he said, "Are Moshe and his family still all right?"

"Yes, but I see little of them. Perhaps, you can visit with him after dark."

"I will."

But before doing this, we had a hearty dinner and shared our family's company. I was happy to see my little brother again. Though he was just barely toddling, his presence was becoming larger in my life. I sat and played with him while my parents talked in muffled tones.

After dark, my father and I went to the barn. "Moshe, Moshe, are you here?" My father asked. We heard the door in the floor of the barn being raised, and Moshe stepped up. "Joseph, so good to see you!"

"You too. Are you doing okay?"

"Yes, thank you again for your hospitality. I have no words."

"I know. We all are doing what we can."

Moshe looked at me and said, "And you, Mitchell, you

look bigger now," he said as he hugged me. I felt his beard tickling my chin, and I playfully pulled it as I often had.

He laughed, but even in the darkness of the barn, I could see his eyes were troubled. Turning to my father he said, "Joseph, I am afraid we are going to have get out of Poland. It is too dangerous for all of us."

"I know. Where you going to go?"

"I think we will try to make it to Switzerland and from there to England."

"That sounds good."

"You know, Moshe, that beard is going to have to go."

"I know," he said with sadness echoing in his voice.

My mother had told us that the German SS were searching people's houses for Jews. She said that they were also taking able-bodied Polish people to dig trenches for the army.

My father told this to Moshe and then said, "I have some ideas of how to keep your presence a secret, but I think we should go pretty soon. I can go with you, as far as the border, if you would like?"

"You don't have to do that. You have done so much already."

"It is nothing. You are my friend."

My father gathered manure from the stalls and spread it over the door to the cellar. "This will confuse the dogs," he told me. Satisfied that he had done what he could inside, he went outside and moved our beehives close to the tunnel's exit. This opening was covered with heavy brush, but my father just wanted to be sure.

However, because this was still winter, the bees were not active, and we hoped it would be enough. Moshe had a few jewels and some money saved, and he wanted my dad to hide them. Father dug a small hole under one of the beehives and hid the glass jar containing these items and then moved the beehive over them again. While it was not the best hiding place, it was convenient in case Moshe's family had to leave quickly.

"Mitchell, Moshe and his family will be leaving soon."

"The news devastated me. I had become attached to these people with their small smiles and kindness. But with everything I had seen and done in the last few months, I simply accepted this new reality. It is difficult to have one's world turned so severely. Everything we thought we understood was cast into uncertainty. Even such simple things as friendships and doing nice things for each other were open to question. I liked the way Moshe's family treated us with respect. As a young boy, being shown such respect by adults is a rare thing. I simply could not understand why the Germans were torturing and killing these people. I knew this was wrong. The Jewish people I knew had always been kind to me.

Nothing I had learned in my life could be applied to this. I guess the only other thing to think about was that the Germans seemed to hate everyone who was not German. I knew they were also imprisoning and persecuting Polish people, even though many Poles had joined with the Germans to persecute the Jews. With the hatred coming from others in town, it was not that difficult to understand. There was, at that time, a natural tension between Jews and Christians. In our village, the Catholic Church did little to quell this animosity, and it festered.

The winter continued, and we did the best we could to survive. There were times when there simply was no food to either buy or steal. We managed to get by though it was extremely difficult to do so.

In our lives, there are times that bring on a renewal of the soul; spring is one of these. As the dark days of winter passed, we should have begun feeling the renewal of the seasons. But we did not.

Living a life of deprivation can do that to a person. Our situation with Moshe's family was becoming more desperate. My father often said that he longed for spring so that he could help them to Switzerland. He did not think that traveling in the winter with a woman and two small children was a good thing to do. It was too cold, and the danger was too great. But as the warm winds of spring began to blow, both Moshe and my father knew the time was at hand.

By this time, the Germans were occupying all of Poland, as well as other small European nations. In truth, we had become used to their presence. But we could never accept this as being right.

The cruelty of the Germans was becoming more widely known, if not understood. We knew that they had built mammoth concentration camps such as Treblinka, the closest one to us. But others, such as Auschwitz, Lublin, and Torun were also nearby. And although these larger camps are those that everyone remembers, it is important to understand that every small town had their own concentration camp built to solve the so called "Jewish Problem." Normal people did not accept these as being right. But there was little we could do.

As the spring dissipated into the month of June and the reports of the Germans increasing their activity in searching for Jews reached beyond rumor, my father and Moshe decided that it was time they moved.

I did not go with my father on this journey. They left at night through the tunnel and walked in the woods toward the Plodownica, a small river that flowed into a larger river and eventually led to the Baltic. We did not know when to expect my father to return. Days turned into weeks, and still he was not back. We were getting worried. I remember seeing my mother at the kitchen table, staring into the backyard. I knew she was praying. I could feel her concern.

One day, Father just appeared.

When he returned, he brought a newspaper. In the newspaper was a picture of Pope Pius XII, blessing the German soldiers and cannons. He was shocked. I can always remember him showing me that picture and saying, "Look, son, the Pope is blessing the German soldiers and their cannons."

My father had decided that we should move to America, but he had no means to make this happen. He had asked my mother to come with him as he led Moshe's family, but she had refused. My father thought that we could also get to the USA via Switzerland. But we still could not locate my sister, and we would not leave without her.

My father only accompanied Moshe's family to the border where they said goodbye. I have never seen Moshe and his family again. I pray that they made it safely to England, but of this I am less than sure.

Almost as soon as Father returned, several German Gendarmes, along with the SS, came to the house looking for him. When he opened the door, they approached him with guns drawn and screamed, "Where have you been? You have been hiding Jews, haven't you?"

"No, I'm an American citizen, and I wouldn't take a chance jeopardizing my return to America with my family."

This answer did not satisfy the men, and one of the SS officers kicked my father in the stomach, knocking him to the ground. "Liar!" he screamed. Another SS man took the butt of his rifle and hit my father viciously in the face. The blood flowed almost immediately, and he fell to the ground. We watched in horror as he was jerked to his feet and led away.

Chapter 10

I was shocked and beside myself with grief. My father, tall and strong, had always been a pinnacle of strength. To see him bloodied, arrested, and taken away affected me deeply. I felt both helpless and hopeless. Helpless because there was nothing that I could do to get my father away from these people; hopeless because I was unsure that anyone could do anything.

My dad and I had done everything together. In my eyes, from my now eight-year-old perspective, he was greatest person on earth. Simply, my father, my hero—the man who knew everything and who could right all wrongs—was gone. Taken from me by the hated Nazis.

We were not sure where he had been taken, although later we heard that he was in a slave labor camp at Allenstein.

Now there were only the three of us: my mother, little brother Andrew, and me. And though they were there for me, they failed to ease the pain of my father's absence. I felt alone and abandoned. It was a terrible loss, and I was depressed for many, many days, sleeping in my room and mumbling when I was asked something. I prayed as hard as I could for my father's release and for this nightmare to end.

Although she was a strong woman, my mom cried often. The truth is that she had her hands full with Andrew and me. For all of us, this adjustment of not having my father around was difficult. It was compounded by worry about his safety.

In war, one of the first things to break down is the structure of traditional roles assigned to men, women and even children. Today, with our modern living standard, this is hard to explain. One important aspect of my father's absence was that he couldn't provide for us. If we needed something, it was up to us to get it. Instead of just waiting for the food to appear magically, we had to find a way to survive.

I began to raid the German army's wagons at night more often. As a small boy, I could get into places that an older person could not. This ability served me well as I raided the wagons for food and anything else we might use. I had no feelings about stealing from them. From my perspective, they were the enemy, and I simply did not care.

I was getting more and more adept at stealing. There was little choice. To be caught would mean certain imprisonment and possibly even death. This knowledge can help to make your footsteps lighter and your mind sharper. Many times I went on foraging expeditions without my mother being aware of where I was going or what I was doing.

I could certainly see her point of view; her husband was, at the very least, locked in prison. For all she knew he might have been killed already. There certainly had been enough sadness in our family already. My grandfather was most likely dead. My aunt was imprisoned in a work camp outside of Moscow. My sister was missing, and more. So many friends had simply disappeared that the entire world had taken on a color of deep sadness.

But on the other hand, we had to be able to survive. My mother was still nursing Andrew, and I saw her losing weight consistently. I wanted to provide for my family the best I could. My father had things he could do. But he was no longer there. I had things I could do, and I did them willingly.

At this time we had the one cow, two chickens, and a rooster. The seasons had changed by this time, and it was winter again, the winter of 1940. Because of the weather I not only had to provide for my family, I had to find grain for the chickens if we wanted an occasional egg. Luckily, my father had the foresight to prepare mounds of hay for the cow to eat before the Germans had taken him. My job, even before he was taken, was to feed the chickens, the cow, and keep their pens clear of manure. I continued doing this.

If I could manage to steal a couple of loaves of German bread, it helped. I started to develop even more stealth in my evening expeditions. The Germans were aware that the local people were stealing, and they would set traps for those people who were taking their food. I learned, after observing several others get caught, what to look for. I would walk by the trucks and try to see what was available during the daylight hours. I would pretend that I was not particularly interested in what they had, all the while doing an inventory with my peripheral vision.

Since Baranowo was a small town, I knew that they were watching me. This made it necessary to travel to other towns to see what I could steal. My mother hated me doing this, but she took the food I stole willingly. In all honesty, the choice was to either eat it or starve. We preferred to survive. The food that I stole was the only way that we were surviving, and she knew it.

The days and nights were cold. I took it upon myself to go to the nearby pine forest and fill up sack after sack of pine needles and drag home branches as large as I could carry for the fire. This was good honest work, and I did it willingly. So, as long as my strength held up, I did it. The problem was that I was becoming weaker. This pain, the pain of hunger, is the worst pain imaginable, because it is so easily solved. It is not like a pain from an injury, though it hurts just as bad. The most painful part of it is that it is so easy to cure, *if* there is food around. It is a great sadness. I know what it means to be hungry. When I think back on my experiences through the war years, hunger is the omnipresent memory.

Even at eight years old I harbored a growing hatred and

contempt for the Germans. They were, in my mind, evil. The many things I had witnessed had hardened my heart to them. Whether it was the young woman with the baby on the train, the mass graves, the public beating of Jews, or the beating and arrest of my father, I had seen enough to convince me of their nature.

A man named Stolarczyk from the Underground approached me as I walked the streets of Baranowo one day. He was in the doorway of a shop and gestured for me to come. He asked me to deliver messages and do some small spying for him. In return for my doing this, he would find my father and break him out of prison. Even though I did not want to do these things, for the chance of having my father released I was willing to do most anything. I agreed to try. But as I said this, I was not certain that there was a lot that I could do. He began to train me to be his eyes and ears.

I guess the main reason that I was reluctant to join the Underground was that my father had often expressed a wish to remain neutral. He had told me that joining one side or the other could jeopardize his chances of returning to the United States with us. He explained that since there was no declared war between the nation of Germany and the United States, he should be able to get us to his home. By being involved in efforts to oppose the Germans, he believed that he might ruin our chances to go to his home.

His position confused me, for while he said this aloud, he secretly kept Moshe's family in our barn and did many other things that were not approved by our German occupiers. It was a position that I did not really understand. I had to make a decision. I agreed to be trained and offer whatever help I could to the Underground.

When the training began, it was simple enough. Stolarczyk and I would stand on the second or third floor of a building. He would instruct me to look out of the window at the street below for five seconds, and then he would take me away from the window. From this brief encounter, I had to tell him how many Germans I had seen, what kind of uniforms they wore, how many officers, what kinds of weapons they were carrying, what they looked like, and many different things. We practiced repeatedly until I became quite good at observing details and reporting.

I really didn't want to work for these people, but I missed my dad. If only he were here, I thought; he would know what to do. I also knew this was war, and choosing the right course is not always easy. But there are times when you simply cannot take too much time in deciding what to do. You just had to do what you felt was the right thing.

So, without my mother's knowledge, and at eight years old, I joined the Underground. Mom needed me for different chores, like taking care of Andrew while she had other things to do, helping with the animals, and such. I know that she was getting suspicious about what I was doing when I was gone for long periods of time, but I continued with my activities.

I tried to allay her fears, but continued working for the Underground in the faint hope that my father would be released. I did not know that this would happen; I only wished it would. All of these decisions were confusing to a young boy. I often prayed for my father's deliverance so that he could make these decisions for me.

One nearly cloudless evening, as I walked into the barn, I heard my name called in the dark. It was my dad! I cried out, "Dad" in disbelief and a little confusion. He ran to me, grabbed and hugged me. He held me for long moments while our tears fell together. I could feel my heart pounding in my chest. The sense of relief I felt in his strong embrace was enough to give me a warm sense of security and happiness. I hugged him back—as strongly as I could. He gave me a harmonica that he had gotten for me somewhere as we embraced. He did not need to give me a gift; his presence was enough. But even this would soon be gone.

"Mitchell, you must go and get your mother and Andrew. I cannot stay, but I want to see them before I go"

"Why do you have to go, Dad?"

"I escaped from the camp; the Germans will be looking for me. I am afraid they might even be coming here."

I ran back to the house. My feet were so light I doubt that I even touched the snow. My mother was sitting at the table, where she often sat. I ran to her and breathlessly panted, "Mom, Dad is in the barn, and he wants to see you and Andrew."

Her face lit up. Smilingly she said, "Mitchell, watch Andrew." I did so willingly.

In a few minutes she came back to get Andrew so Dad could see him before he left. "Did your father tell you that he escaped from the prison camp at Allenstein?"

"Yes, he did."

"Mitchell, the Nazis will be looking for him. You must never tell anyone that your father has been here. Understand?"

I nodded and followed her to the barn. When we got there, my father looked at Andrew for a few seconds; he kissed and hugged him with tears in his eyes. Then he hugged my mom and me. We had all lost weight, so his long arms almost wrapped around us easily. With tears in his eyes, my father left through the cellar and the tunnel.

After he had left, I remembered how he had confused the German dogs and got the cow manure and put it over the boards at the entrance to the cellar. Now, I spread manure, hoping it would protect my father. With all the excitement I almost forgot to feed the cow, so I got big wads of hay from the haystack and threw it into her feeding bin.

Chapter 11

In our region, the most feared German was a local commandant named Placek. Placek was an ugly man: completely bald, a pot belly, and a calm sneer on his face that could almost be mistaken for a smile. There had been many incidents involving this man. His heritage was half German and half Pole, though he was a leader in the Gestapo now. He could speak both German and Polish, and therefore, was invaluable to the Germans. He often would disguise himself as a simple Polish farmer and try to find out what the people were thinking. I do not believe that this actually worked in Baranowo, but it did work in other places where he was not as well-known.

When someone was wanted, they sent Placek to get them. Although technically Placek was not in charge, I think the German Commissioner actually feared this man who had no redemptive qualities. Often, the people wanted for questioning would try to run. He would shoulder his rifle and shoot them without a thought. He gave no warning; it was just naked murder. His taunting half-smile smirk would light with each pull of the trigger. His pleasure in this malevolent activity was evident. It was as if he were hunting some animal in the forest or shooting clay pigeons at a practice range.

In the summer of 1940, Placek and some of his men went into the tall pine forest on the end of town by the blacksmith shop to hunt. It was not unusual for the people, even those in authority, to hunt at that time. Food was in short supply all over, and taking a stag or a brace of rabbits could certainly help to fill anyone's larder.

On this particular summer day, two young Polish girls,

fourteen years old, were in the forest picking mushrooms. I am sure they were giggling and laughing the way young girls do. They meant no harm and were certainly doing nothing wrong. I knew the girls from church and they were nice. An idyllic scene: young girls in a calm forest pursuing a fun activity in the golden light of summer. This scene would soon be shattered by the evil of man.

Now, it is hard for me to understand why, but I guess contempt for people will allow you to pursue whatever activity seems right to you. Obviously these men were overcome by lust as they approached the young girls. Making lewd suggestions, they began to sexually fondle them. I am certain that rape was on their minds. After all, what could anyone do? They were the law.

The girls screamed and tried to run. Placek calmly raised his gun to a shooting position, aimed it carefully, and without the slightest bit of remorse, pulled the trigger. His shot hit one of the young girls at close range. The shot severed her arm near the shoulder, and both girls screamed even more loudly.

The men accompanying this monster were aware that they were committing a great evil and began moving out of the wood taking the hated Placek with them. The two young girls were abandoned, even though one was grievously injured.

The young girl who had not been shot was trying to help her friend when a local farmer, having heard the shots, arrived in his horse-drawn wagon. Seeing what had happened, he rushed the girls onto the wagon and began driving toward town.

The farmer had his hands full; he was trying to calm the girls, drive the horses, and stop the bleeding. We did not have a doctor in our small town, but we had a good veterinarian named Feltzer. The farmer took the girl to his house as quickly as he could.

When he arrived, the vet did his best to help the girls. He managed to get the bleeding controlled. The injured girl would live. Word spread of the incident, and people began gathering in front of the church. You have to remember that the church was the focal point of the people's lives so this was a natural extension of their offense.

This incident had offended people deeply. As a mob, they began moving toward the police station calling, "Placek—We want justice."

Another collaborator—we never knew who exactly they were—informed the Germans, and they quickly set up a machine gun on the road to the police station. When the people approached, the Germans began firing into the crowd, firing without warning or mercy.

The carnage was terrible. Ten people died immediately, while scores of others were critically wounded. Those people who died that day had only wanted to express their outrage at a bad man.

I do not believe that my town ever recovered from that violent event. The wound the Germans had inflicted went much deeper than the dead bodies littering the road that day. Certainly they had killed ten people, but they had also thrust a dagger deeply into our hearts.

That evening, after seeing my father for those precious few minutes, I was trying to find understanding in a world that seemed to defy this. So many things had gone wrong that I was beginning to lose my ability to perceive the world. Everything I thought I knew was now changed. My confusion was overwhelming, like quicksand that sucked me deeper with every turn.

I wanted my father there to explain the world to me. I could not get the image of the soldier killing the young woman and her infant at the train station out of my mind. I did not understand. To me, these people were just like me. I could not understand why the Germans and their Polish collaborators were persecuting them. In truth, their only crime seemed to be that they were Jewish, and this made no sense. I had been taught that we are all children of God and made in his image. Such things as religious beliefs did not seem to override the distorted view of the world that had a stranglehold on the Nazis.

I had so many questions to ask my father, but now he was gone again. I felt badly that I did not even get a chance to tell him about my delivering messages for the Underground. I would have liked to ask his permission.

I was also wondering if my delivering messages had caused someone to help him escape. But I did not think so. He had mentioned no one's help in escaping and said that he had escaped alone. If someone would have helped him, he would have been aware of my part in this and thanked me. This only added to my confusion.

In the early morning, when it was still dark and cold, the Gendarmes, led by Placek's Gestapo, came to our house. We were rocked from our beds when they kicked in the door. I can never get that sound out of my mind. The peace of the morning shattered by the hobnailed boot of the Gestapo. They kicked in the doors of the bedrooms and ripped us out of our beds and threw us into the sitting room. My mother was crying, I was frightened and clung tightly to her. Her arm holding me close was reassuring. But this was not to last.

The Gestapo began by ripping me away from my mother and then, with their fists protected by tight black leather gloves, they began hitting her. They struck her in the stomach and the face until she fell to the ground; then they kicked her, all the while shouting, "Where is your husband? We know he escaped and came here. Where is he?" Each question was punctuated with another blow until my mother was bleeding from her lips and nose and was crying on the floor of our home.

My father had not told us where he was going, other than to the forest to hide. There was nothing we could tell them. We knew that it was possible that he would try to make his way to Grabownica, but we did not know this. As I watched my mother being beaten, rage overcame me, and I tried to help. I ran toward Placek with my fists clenched tightly. A Gestapo Officer grabbed me and held me tight. His eyes never met mine; he simply watched the scene unfold before him while keeping me in check with an iron grip.

When no information was forthcoming, we were roughly grabbed and taken to the police station. My mother was taken to one room and I was taken to another. Some of the Gestapo took my mother and left me with their commandant, Placek, the pig. He took a bullwhip, long and braided, and began striking me and screaming, "Where is your father?"

I ran about the room as if I were a rat trying to escape the whistling whip, but it did little good. He continued to strike me until my shirt was in tatters and I was bleeding from my back and arms. Finally, seeming to tire of the chase, he grabbed my hair and dragged me over to a bench near the wall.

The room was being remodeled and there was a wooden carpenter's vise attached to the bench. Watching my eyes, he took my thumb and placed it in the vise. With that half-smile smirk that we hated so, he watched my eyes as he slowly turned the handle, squeezing my thumb tighter and tighter. All the while smiling broadly.

When it was tightly held and the pain was almost unbearable, he struck me across the face with his open hand—back and forth—as he screamed, "Where is your father?" I did not answer. I could not answer. I did not know.

The tears were bursting from my eyes. He turned the

handle tighter with a smile. My thumb was mangled now. Blood was bursting from the nail. He continued hitting me and screaming, "Where is your father?"

When I passed out, I was glad. I wanted to die. Anything to take the pain away. My entire body was bruised and bloodied from the whipping, and now the pain in my thumb was mind-numbing. But when I woke again, the beating continued. "Please don't hurt me no more," I cried. I longed for a quick death—the pain was that severe. The pain had driven my mind deeper and deeper within me; I lost all coherence. I would have done anything to stop the pain, but I could not respond. After I began moving in and out of consciousness, I don't remember too much. I know that he continued beating me and tightening the vise, but I am not sure what I did or did not say. I was completely disoriented, shaking, and sobbing. I was glad that I kept passing out.

Chapter 12

Apparently, even Placek had limits to his endurance. When he tired, the beating finally stopped. I had no idea how long I had been in that room being tortured. Time had refused to hold meaning for me. It could have been fifteen minutes or several hours; I just did not know. The pain was so intense and unending, my mind refused to contemplate such things as time. I was even more troubled by the fact that I had no recollection of what I had said, or did not say. Finally, I was released from the vise and collapsed on the floor. When I came to Placek had a hot poker in his hand. He sat on my chest, and when he was sure I couldn't move, he touched my right arm with the hot iron. I passed out again.

One of the other policemen must have taken me to a cell where I was thrown onto the floor. I slept in that cell, even though the pain was almost unbearable. I remember waking during the night in the cold darkness because I had moved and touched my thumb. In truth, I did not even want to look at it and blessed the darkness that prohibited me from doing so. Though my thumb throbbed and the pain was constant, I was also aware that I was still alive; this gave me a shard of hope for the future. With all of the death I had seen and the German's lack of mercy, at least this was something.

I was awakened before dawn and thrown into the back of a truck without sides. The Gendarmes took me over rough roads to an indoctrination school located at the Allenstein Complex. The Germans had built a school, a labor camp, and the concentration camp here. Surrounded by barbed wire fences, the complex was punctuated with machine gun nests placed where they had a clear view to shoot, in case anyone should try to escape.

I was assigned a bed in one of the barracks with other Polish kids. The Germans then began to work on our minds with the object of making us into good Nazis. Life there was unlike any school I had ever known. In the morning, this Nazi officer came into the room and woke us by screaming, "Heil, Hitler!" We were taught to raise our right hand and scream back, "Heil, Hitler."

If any of the boys refused to do this, or did not do it in the proper way, they were taken away and punished. Punishment to the Germans was designed to leave a lasting impression, a kind of branding iron mark to the psyche that touches all the senses in a permanent way. When you see your bunkmate taken away and returned beaten terribly and nearly dead, his body wracked with pain and covered with bruises, it stimulates your enthusiasm for returning the Nazi salute.

I remember how badly I felt, dressed in my shabby rags, when they would come in with their uniforms freshly laundered and pressed. Their high leather boots polished to a bright gleam had the effect of making us seem to be less than they were.

I had thoughts of not cooperating. In truth, though I was a young boy, my hatred for them ran deep. I would have liked to tell them to go to Hell. But I did not. My body was still covered with bruises from the beating and stripes from the whip. My thumb was useless to me, swollen and blackened. It throbbed constantly and I gritted my teeth every time I touched it. I did what they asked.

Once we were roused out of bed, we dressed in the clothes provided. It was probably a good thing, as the clothes I had on when they took me from my home were tattered and bloodied. The shirts they gave us had a large, red "P" on the back. That "P" was for Polish. We were taken to a sort of mess hall and fed whatever meager food they had to spare.

Usually a thin gruel of some sort that tasted awful and a crust of old bread. It was disgusting, but at least it was edible.

When we finished, we were herded into a classroom where we were expected to pay close attention to the Nazi teacher. He would rise and address us, in perfect Polish, about the wonder and correctness of the Germans ruling Poland. I listened without expression, but all I could see when the man talked, was that poor mother and her infant killed, without mercy or remorse, at the train station. I did not argue, but I did not listen either. In truth, nothing they could have said would have erased that scene from my consciousness.

After they harangued us for hours, we were taken outside to work. The work was hard. But with the constant threat of beatings and torture hanging over us, we did our best. The pain in my thumb made this difficult, but I tried.

This man was not our only teacher; on other occasions, a young boy would come in to address us. He was resplendent in full Nazi regalia. His brown shirt was clean and neatly pressed. His armband in red, with the swastika displayed prominently, stands out in my mind. I guess their idea was that if we heard their argument from someone our own age, we would be more receptive. It did not work with me. Again, I had seen too much to ever listen to them. This young boy would explain that there was no Poland anymore and furthermore, there never had been. He told us that he used to be like us, but he had seen the wisdom of the Nazis and had converted. I simply dismissed him.

When he was done speaking, the instructor ordered us outside and we were taught to sing Nazi songs while we marched to our work details. To this day, I can remember the words to, "Deutschland, Deutschland, Liber ales."

That is not to say that I let my feelings show. I did not. I became a willing little Nazi. I had been beaten and tortured, and if they wanted me to act in such a manner to avoid further episodes, I certainly would. Experience is a stern teacher.

Life was gruesome in this camp. When we were working outside, some of the young children of the Nazis would come along and, as their parents watched approvingly, kick us and beat us with sticks. I watched this happen many times, but I never understood it. How could a parent allow their children to act in such a manner?

In the evening, when we were alone, we would occasionally talk. Mostly, this was a time where we lamented our situation. But one night a boy, whom I knew only slightly, told us some news. He told us that a German commandant named Placek, from Baranowo had been severely injured. This man was so evil that he was legendary, and his reputation for cruelty had spread far beyond our town. The boy told us that Placek used to practice—with another Nazi—jumping the fence surrounding the Rynek, the marketplace by our house.

He treated his horse no better than he treated anyone else. I had often seen him doing this and I listened attentively as he told that the horse had balked at the fence one day and threw Placek to the ground in front of him. The horse, seeing his chance for revenge on its hateful master, reared up and came down on Placek's chest with his forefeet. The horse continued doing this until Placek was severely injured. I laughed. Considering how much he had hurt me, I could not help myself. It made me feel that there was hope after all. I slept well that night with a smile gracing my lips.

As I said, I became a willing little Nazi; I was soon less-watched because they believed that I was with them. One day, just before we were to be returned to the barracks, I saw my chance. The fence was not that far away. I ran. I have always been a fast runner, and I never ran as fast as I did that day.

When I reached the fence, I dove under it and continued running as quickly as I could. I did not even look behind me; I just ran and ran. It was early springtime and the air of freedom filled my lungs—I kept running.

I did not know what to do or where to go, but being free of that camp gave me an exuberance I'd never known before. The work was hard, and I wanted so much to be reunited with my family that the thought was overwhelming. I slept in the forest that night. The next day I decided to try to make my way to my Godfather's house, which was in that region.

I had been to their house several times before, and I managed to find it that day. I waited until it was dark. I approached the door and knocked tentatively.

When the door was opened slightly, I saw Kuzia, my Godfather. He smiled and asked, "Mitchell, how did you come to be here?"

"I was being held at Allenstein, but I ran away."

"Come in, come in and be welcome."

They welcomed me into their small house and it felt good to find a place that reminded me of my own home. I stayed with them. They were wonderful people. They had a boy about my age, also named Mitchell, and we became fast friends. But it was not my home. I ached for my family.

News, even though the Nazis tried to suppress it, did have a way of making its way through the population. In the early spring of 1941, we heard that there was a new police force in Baranowo. I heard again that Placek had been wounded severely; that made me smile once more.

I decided that it was time I moved on to try and find my way back home. With the snow mostly gone, it was easier to move without detection. When the world is all white, a person stands out against the background. Now, with the snow-cover greatly diminished, there was a good chance I could move without being seen. Besides, if I went soon, the ice would still be in the Plodownica River, and I could cross without having to try the bridges, which were constantly manned by the Germans.

Even from where we were, we could tell that something big was happening. The Germans seemed distracted and busy, as men and machines moved through the area on their way to attack their allies, the Russians.

I was going to be nine years old soon, and I wanted to be home. I told Kuzia and his family that I was leaving to go home. They looked concerned, but they did not stop me. I hugged them tightly and they said repeatedly, "God bless you and good luck." Both of them hugged me back. After saying goodbye to their son, I left on my journey home.

Chapter 13

In the wake of a long life, it is hard for me to remember how I did the things that I did. The spring of 1941 was making ready to change the landscape of Poland, as it did faithfully every year. But somehow, even that could not calm the anxiety I felt. I was a mere child walking in the deep Polish forest with the Germans moving all about me—Germans who would kill me in an instant without an adult. Physically, I was still a young boy. Mentally, I had aged considerably.

I walked quietly, as my father had taught me, and tried to keep from view. It was obvious that something important was happening. The noise of the trucks and other mechanized equipment moving east clung in the air like a funeral shroud. I tried my best to stay away from the activity, keep my feet moving, and continue walking toward my home.

I crossed the river without incident and neared Baranowo in the late afternoon. On the outskirts of town, in the portion of town we called Poswiecie, I saw my father's cousins working in the field. When I saw them, the heaviness in my feet vanished, and I ran toward them shouting their names.

They welcomed me warmly and hugged me. I immediately asked, "Do you have any news of my family?"

"Your father is staying in your mother's parents' house in Podorle."

I knew where that was. As soon as I said goodbye, I started running toward the outskirts of Baranowo.

I couldn't wait to see my father; my heart was pounding with excitement. I ran hard and fast. My father was special to me, but he was special to other people, too. There was something about him that people liked. He had a good sense of humor and smiled easily. That, and he had an inner strength that he seemed to be able to give to others. I missed that strength and wanted, more than anything, to tap this.

I arrived after dark and moved onto the property as quietly as I could. I did not want to alarm anyone inside of the house or anyone that may have been watching the outside. The house was built out of logs, and there was an old barn on the property. I saw a slight amount of smoke coming out of the chimney, and flashes of light through the chinks in the logs. When I got closer to the house, I walked to the door and knocked quietly.

My dad opened the door. When he saw me, he grabbed and hugged me, and kept on kissing me and calling my name. I hugged him back, and clung to him tenaciously for long minutes. Finally, we broke our embrace and I asked, "What about Mom and Andrew?"

"I've heard that she is in a small camp in Torun. Andrew is probably being brainwashed by the Nazis"

"Is there any way we can get them out?"

"I've been trying, but it's hard in these times." He lamented, but added with more hope, "I've been in contact with the Underground. They have agreed to try and find her and help her to escape. If this doesn't work, I can ask your uncle in Ostroleka. You remember him? The one who's a conductor on the railroad."

"Yes, I remember him, but I thought you said that he was a collaborator?"

"I have heard that, but I don't believe it. He's a good man."

We talked for hours. It had been so long and so much had happened in our lives that we needed to share our experiences. The night seemed to evaporate in the warm presence of my father. Before we knew it, it was early in the morning.

"Did you know that the Germans have burned all of the books? It is now a crime to own a book. But I guess it is another law I'm breaking," he said as he swept his hand toward the books lining the shelves.

"Aren't you worried about them?"

"Of course I am. But I need these books to teach you to read. I have been praying for your return, and now the Lord has heard my prayers. I will teach you again, but right now we have to go and get your mother."

"When?"

"As soon as possible. I want her and Andrew away from these people."

I was scared for them. I knew what the Germans were like and I could imagine all kinds of bad things happening to them. When I thought of my little brother, I was troubled. I still had the terrible vision of the little Jewish infant at the station, so tiny and helpless, flashing through my mind. The image of the mother and child invading my world was a regular occurrence by now.

This incident had dwelt in my mind, and the child's mother—I'll never forget her eyes, half pleading, half angry, full of pain. She was so confused. She had looked in disbelief with the pain in her sunken eyes showing that the loss of her child was unbearable. These strangers had become like family. After all, they could have been my mother, my brother.

I just could not understand; how could the soldiers do this? How could they snuff that little infant and his mother out of existence forever, just because they were Jewish and hungry? How could they do this, so cold and calculating. Did they not answer to God?

In the morning, we had kasza, a warm cereal served with

milk, for breakfast. While we were eating, my father said, "Mitchell, your mom and I are going to have another baby in June, maybe a girl this time!"

"Great! How do you know when?"

"She told me, before she was taken."

"Do you think we can get her back?"

"I know that I will do anything I can to make certain that we do."

My face lit up with excitement, and my sister Irene came to mind. It had been about two years since I had seen Irene; I still missed her terribly.

My father turned away and I studied him carefully. I noticed that he had changed. He seemed older somehow and his sense of humor was nearly gone. While he used to laugh all of the time and enjoy life, this seemed to have been taken from him. But I guess it had been for all of us. War and the Germans were simply not very funny.

My father had told me that my grandfather had suffered a terrible death in the Russian prison and of others in my family dying or missing. It had been a year or two since I had seen my aunts or my uncles. He told me that some had been killed in the Warsaw uprising. I had not seen my mom or Andrew for a long time, but dad was here with me now, and surely he would know what to do.

"Dad, who have you been talking with in the Underground?"

"Why?"

"While you were gone, I did some things for them."

"Like what?"

"There was this man, Stolarczyk, who recruited me. He told me that he would help you to escape. I gather he didn't."

"No, he did not. What did you do for them?"

"Mostly little stuff. I used to carry messages for him. Sometimes I watched the street for soldiers."

"Mitchell, you should not have done this. It was very dangerous."

"What was I supposed to do, Dad? He said he would get you out of prison. I wanted that more than anything."

"But it was dangerous. Is that all you did?"

"No. . . I guess not."

"What else did you do?" His face clouded over and his lower lip quivered as he asked the question.

"One night, me and another boy snuck into the Germans' camp and stole guns."

"Tell me."

"One morning, when I went to the forest to see Stolarczyk as I was supposed to, he introduced me to another boy, Wlacek. He was about my age, but he was bigger than me. 'I want you to get two Lugers.' He handed me a little knife, and told me it was razor-sharp. 'Go to the old school; they will show a movie to the German soldiers. They don't pay much attention to kids, and it's going to be very crowded there. The soldiers usually stand up when they watch a movie. When the soldiers are watching the movie, simply take the guns. If they have them snapped in their holsters, you will have to cut the straps. Use the knife.'

"That evening we went to the school. The movie had started already. We walked in through a large open door. It was dark inside except for light from the projector. Regular German soldiers didn't pay attention to small kids, so I picked the darkest spot, and I started shoving through, zipping the gun off with the razor. I put it in my big pocket and carefully moved through the soldiers, to the door, and out of the building."

"What? Mitchell, what were you thinking of?"

"You."

"Son, I don't ever want you to do this sort of thing again!"

"I won't. But I was trying to help."

"I know, but this is not your war. Not your fight. It is not right. I would rather be in their prison than endanger you, do you understand this?"

"Yes, I guess I do. But we all have to do the best that we can, don't we?"

"Yes, but I simply do not want you to endanger your life needlessly."

I realized he was right. After he gave me a long speech, I promised him that I would not do something that foolish again. When he was finished, he told me to stay put and that he would be back soon.

While he was gone, I thought about what he had told me, and also other thoughts wandered through my mind. I looked at my life such as it was at this time. I remembered the time before the war, when I couldn't even imagine a world without my family. I thought how lucky we were to have so many choices; there weren't any choices now. It seemed so long ago. Yet, these memories from before the war eased my tortured mind and relieved my grief a bit.

In the past, my sense of humor helped somewhat, but I seemed to have lost that. Whether I was awake or asleep, the horrible pictures were etched behind my eyelids—pictures of torture, suffering and the deaths of so many people, even little children. I struggled with my faith in God. I didn't understand his reasoning, and sometimes I would get angry with him. But I continued to pray and ask for understanding. I am not sure my prayers were answered, but I was surviving. That was the best that this lost-and-found child of almost nine could hope for in that time and place of sorrows.

Chapter 14

While I waited for my father to return that evening, I prayed. As an adult, I have come to accept that prayers are not always answered. But as a child, I did not understand why God could permit these awful men to exist. Their evil was apparent, and I knew it. If I, a child, knew it, then must God not surely know it?

I tried to focus my mind on the present, but the past kept interrupting me. I closed my eyes and remembered what I had witnessed on my way back to Baranowo. I had been walking in the still forest when I heard the sound of machine guns and screams. It was not very far from where I was, so I moved quietly in that direction. I guess I wanted to know if there was something there I should be concerned with.

Through the deep woods, I saw another mass grave filled with people, freshly shot, and moaning. I hid in the woods and watched. One baby, an infant, was still alive! I watched the SS man go to the baby; rather than waste a bullet, he took the butt of his rifle and viciously struck the infant in the head, smashing its skull.

When he left, I went over to the grave. I am not sure why I did this. I guess I wanted to see if there was anything I could do to help. Through the mangled bodies of the dying people, I saw the baby. It was still moving. I bent and picked up its tiny arms in my hands. He looked at me with those trusting and pain-filled eyes, and he died. After the infant slipped away, I started running from the mass grave. I had to keep running, because if I had stopped, I would have collapsed under the crushing emotional pain.

I did not understand at that time, and sixty more years of

living has not offered a suitable explanation. This was an abomination against the Lord and his children. Why? I do not understand.

The truth was that we were all becoming animals: killing, stealing food, and ignoring the plight of our fellow humans. But I continued to pray for the safety of my family. My mom, brother, and sister were never far from my mind.

I learned to get through the day in increments of moments. I did not plan for the future, and I tried my best not to dwell on the past—I knew that I could not change what had already occurred. It was the only way I could keep my perspective. These things, these terrible things haunted me, tempted me to give up and just die. But for some reason, I am a survivor. I understand that now. I will do what is necessary, but when I was young and saw the terrible things done to my fellow humans, I wanted to give up.

The hatred of Jews and Polish people was almost unbearable, particularly at my age. I knew it was wrong. My parents had done their best to shield me from the unpleasant side of life until the war started. Now, I knew much more than I wanted to know about the dark side of our existence. I had been thrust into the position of providing for my family when I was a child. I had witnessed gruesome events and experienced beatings and torture at the hands of the German oppressors. It was easy to know, if not to understand, the tenuous nature of our existence.

My parents had taught me to judge people on their deeds and not on something that mattered little, such as what religion they practiced or what language they spoke. However, I found this harder and harder to do. I thought, many times, that there were kids my age somewhere, who were still sleeping with a security blanket. I slept with a gun. I did not think it fair and it bothered me immensely. My mother used to say things like it was all for the best, but I could not accept this simplistic answer anymore. How can the best be terrible pain and incredible hunger?

Occasionally, I would get an overwhelming feeling of hopelessness. I felt that God did not want anything to do with me. At times I wished I knew more about God. Perhaps more knowledge would have helped me to understand better what I saw. I could not grasp the destruction. The starving and defenseless people herded into cattle cars bound for the concentration camps. The mass killings I had seen. The beatings for no reason. It did not make sense to me. How could God justify the Germans killing anyone who was too sick to work? This was as close as I could conceive of to anti-Christian behavior. I had been taught in church to care for those less fortunate or sick.

At this time there were rumors that the Nazis had begun experimenting with children and diseases. I could hardly believe it. I did not think that anyone could be cruel enough to take children and babies and deliberately subject them to infectious diseases! The thought troubled me, and I was afraid to be caught. I could not conceive of being in the hands of the Nazis again. I knew I would do almost anything to prevent this from happening. I asked my father about the non-Christian behavior of the Nazis. Without hesitating he responded, "God does not make war, people do. You cannot blame the Lord for the actions of humans." It was a valuable insight, which I have kept with me ever since. So, I just thanked the Lord for my still being alive.

When my father returned, he told me that the Germans were going to attack Russia. I had noticed the men and machines moving that way on my way home. But my father said it was even stronger than I knew about. It was as if the entire German Army was moving through Poland.

The Germans had little time for small town Poles now, and they left us alone for the most part. Occasionally, they would arrest someone and torture them for information, but even this was less frequent than it had been before. The Underground was increasingly active and bold. They fought the Germans wherever and whenever they could. I knew my father, although not a member of the Underground, helped them sometimes. I never asked him about it. It was better for me not to know. I knew this as well.

Dad and I tried to find my mom and Andrew everywhere we could. The movement of troops and machinery increased at this time; because the Germans were occupied, we had more freedom of movement. But we did not find her. Father was becoming increasingly frantic about my mother. The baby was due in June, and it was now past that date. He was gone more and more frequently. I knew he was making every conceivable contact to find her.

Finally, in the early summer of 1941, the Russians began to attack the Germans. They started by bombing the German camps anywhere they could find them. We saw the Russian planes filling the skies above Baranowo.

The Polish Underground Army and Russian Army became allies, which gave people a little hope. Russian fighter planes dropped leaflets from the air over Baranowo. The leaflets explained that when the planes attacked the Germans, they had no wish to hurt us. If we saw planes, we should wave a white handkerchief. That would permit the pilots and bombardiers to know that we were not with the German Army. Our skies were filled with dogfights between Russian fighters and German bombers. The Russians tried to intercept every bomber and shoot them down.

At last, there was word! My mother was probably being held in a women's labor camp in Torun. While this was not a certainty, Father believed that it could be fairly reliable information. We left nearly immediately.

We walked through the summer woods, sleeping out in the open and trying to avoid any population centers. While the Germans seemed preoccupied, there was no sense in tempting them.

We arrived at the camp on a sunny, beautiful summer's morning at about ten in the morning. We saw the camp and as we were walking toward the gate, the sky was suddenly filled with Russian bombers. We did not know what to do or where to hide. The bombs began falling nearly immediately. My father and I looked around for some sort of shelter. Simply, there was none to be had. The best we could do was lie in a ditch by the side of the road and watch. My father shielded me by lying over me. The weight and nearness of his body felt reassuring, but I was still scared.

The planes attacked the German army posts first, then the bombs rained on the city. People were running everywhere, screaming and looking for shelter. We felt fortunate to have found at least the ditch to hide in. We watched as the gates of the work camp were stormed by the prisoners running for cover.

As we looked, I saw my mother coming. Without hesitation we jumped out of the ditch and ran toward her. She was dragging Andrew by the hand and carrying a baby. When Dad and I hugged them, it seemed like their bodies bent from the hug. My mother was so desperately thin that I could feel nearly every bone. But I hugged her all the more tightly.

We retreated to the ditch as the planes were still flying overhead. We took our white handkerchiefs out and began waving them feverishly. We were crying tears of joy for my mother's return. When the planes flew by without firing a shot, our happiness erupted in still more tears as our bodies pressed together.

When the planes had disappeared into the distant sky, my mother said, "Mitchell, this is your little sister Sophie." She said it with pride, but the fatigue showed on her face. My father gently kissed baby Sophie and said, "Mitchell, welcome your sister with a kiss." I did.

Chapter 15

When the planes left, our joy was complete. Our family sat in the ditch by the side of the road smiling. I still missed Irene and wished she were there to share our joy. I don't know for sure how long we stayed there. It seemed like a long time, but it might have been minutes. Before too long my father said, "I suppose we had better get going; it would not do to be sitting beside the road when the Germans come." I knew it was not even noon on a beautiful summer's day when we left.

Picking up Andrew so we could travel more quickly, my father led the way. My mother carried Sophie and held my hand. It was as if she did not quite believe that I was there, and she needed the assurance of my hand in hers. The feeling was mutual.

We entered the forest the way we had come and began walking. It was nearly dark when we came across some members of the Polish Army. They were staying in a bunker. My father went ahead of us and met with their leader. They talked quietly for a few minutes. I stood by my mother. Finally, my father waved for us to come and we were welcomed.

It was a relief to see some friendly faces, and they gladly shared their food with us. The men cooed at Sophie and were very amicable toward us.

I noticed one boy there, a lad of about eighteen, whom the men seemed to pick on constantly. They did not hurt him, but made him the brunt of many cruel jokes. I did not like the way that they treated him. I left my father's side to sit by my mother. I noticed that the young man sat by himself. He was obviously a Jew, and I was offended by the way he was treated, as if he were less important than the others. This was not the way I had been brought up.

My father talked with the men long after we had made a nest and gone to sleep. I could hear their soft voices. "Why don't you join us? We can find a safe house for your family."

"I can't," my father said. "Besides, I am supporting the Underground in Baronowo." The men seemed to understand. My father then asked, "Do you know this Stolarczyk?" The tension in his voice showed his dislike for the man. He was suspicious of anyone who would put children in jeopardy.

"Yes, a good man. A hero."

"Good. I was afraid he was not."

"Why?"

"He recruited my son to spy for them and to..." He went on to tell them about my experience in stealing the lugers from the German soldiers. I drifted off to sleep and cannot remember any more of the conversation.

The next morning a small contingent of the group accompanied us to the road to Baranowo. It felt reassuring to have the heavily armed men with us, and we walked easily with much less fear than normal. When we reached the road at the edge of the forest, the Germans were waiting.

They began firing immediately. I was scared and looked to my father for direction. He picked up Andrew and took my hand and we ran backwards, so that we could see what the Germans were doing, into the cover of the forest.

Bullets zinged by, crashing through the pine needles and into the trees. When we reached a point some distance into the woods, we turned our backs to the Germans and ran as fast as we could. Most of the members of the Underground who had come with us did the same, all except the young Jewish boy the men had harassed the previous night.

He took his weapon, a heavy machine gun, and after finding a little tussock of ground, set up the gun and began firing at the Germans as they tried to pursue us. The men called for him to come; he refused. He continued firing effectively at the Germans. Shot after shot rang out from his position and the Germans were confused. They were used to firing at unarmed civilians, not brave men who would willingly die to take their lives.

The men stopped when we moved into the forest's outer cloak. They tried to go back to help the young man, but the German fire was too intense. They screamed for him to come, but he refused to retreat.

The young man held the Germans at the road while we escaped into the deeper forest. I heard the leader of the resistance praise the Jewish boy saying, "I don't want to hear one bad word about him. He saved us. Do you understand?" The men nodded and they were glad that he was there to help.

I honestly believe, if there had been a chance, they would have tried to save him. Instead, they let him die, knowing that he had saved our lives by sacrificing his own. It was one of the bravest things I have ever seen. I will never forget his courage and selfless actions.

We took another trail toward Baranowo and safely reached the edge of the forest. This time we walked into the open fields without any trouble. Baranowo was practically surrounded by a forest of great pine trees—the Germans could not watch everywhere. Besides, we had heard from the men that the Germans were very busy with their invasion of Russia, and they really didn't have enough manpower to be overly concerned about the resistance.

As we walked, my father said, "We must have surprised that German Patrol. I don't believe they really wanted to fight. They were probably on their way to Russia."

I thought about this. Then I thought about the young

Jew who had died saving us, so many Christians in the middle of this oppression, and was sad once more.

Walking through the fields, it wasn't long until we arrived in Baranowo. We went back to our house and moved in. Our home. Yes, surely it would always be here. Still, I was surprised to find it waiting to shelter us again. It felt so good to sleep in my own bed, I cannot even describe the feeling.

There were a few hectares of land by the house, but it was too late to plant most crops. Still, we did the best we could. My dad got a cow and a goat from somewhere and moved them into the barn. The goat was milked daily for the baby, the cow for the rest of us. My mother was happy once again, and it showed.

My mom managed to get a few chickens with a rooster and three geese. I was even given the task of taking the cow to the community pasture everyday and watching over her so she would not eat other people's crops. It was as if we had awakened from the nightmare of the past months. If only we could believe it had never happened.

Dad found some books from somewhere and proceeded to tutor me. I had to read to him daily. He helped me hone my reading skills, long neglected by the ruthless distractions of war. He even found an old mathematics book and taught me this as well.

On the north side of town was the pasture and a very small river called Plodownica where I went swimming with other town kids while we watched our animals. The water was so clean I could see the bottom—white sand in some places, dark water in others. After the brutality I had witnessed, the water felt wonderful, uncommonly pure. I enjoyed swimming with the others and being a child. I had almost forgotten those sensations so akin to innocence.

The pasture was large. After a while German soldiers brought their horses there and ordered us to watch them.

What choice did we have?

But I did get to ride the horses, as the other boys did. We rode them bareback, which took some getting used to, but once we learned, it was fun. I picked a medium-sized black mare to ride back to town because she was the fastest. Some of the smaller kids would bring the cows back to town. But we took turns so they could also ride the horses.

The German soldiers stayed out of the open pasture, because every day there were Russian fighter planes in the air, diving and shooting at anything they believed to be a German soldier. It did my heart good to see them hiding in the haystacks while we waved our handkerchiefs at the planes.

In the summer, finding food was not too difficult. There were plenty of fish in the river, and my father and I caught a good number. I could also steal food from the German wagons at night. I was very adept at this, and the Germans never knew they had been robbed until the next day.

About this time a German sergeant named Wagner came to our house and demanded quarters. He took one of the bedrooms for his own and moved in his possessions. No one could say anything about it, but he seemed a decent man. In the time he stayed he never did anything to hurt us. In fact, on occasion he would bring home food from the army kitchen for us. He could not speak Polish, so we had a difficult time talking to him. This would have been okay, but he really liked to talk and would jabber on in German. Though I could not understand him, I got the distinct feeling that he would rather have been home with his family. And although we did not speak the same language, his eyes smiled. That was enough.

I had to watch my brother sometimes, as well as my baby sister Sophie, because Mom often went to different farms, picking tomatoes, digging potatoes, and tying up wheat bales. Many times she came home crying because her feet bled so terribly from stepping on the cut wheat stubs; she had no shoes.

Since we didn't have anything planted of our own, Dad and Mom had to prepare some food for winter. By working for the local farmers, they were given some food. My dad dug a deep hole in the ground, lined it with straw, and buried potatoes in the hole for spring. The ground froze only a couple of feet deep, and the potatoes wouldn't freeze.

In early November, Sergeant Wagner left. His outfit had been reassigned. I believe he was a good man. I never saw him hurt anyone, unlike other Germans; even his attitude was different.

My dad prepared the haystack for the cow and goats for the winter and cut some firewood for both cooking and keeping warm during the long, terrible winters. I helped to get the wood from the pine forest, and I raked piles of pine needles and brought them home to burn in the winter.

Chapter 16

Not far from our house, just across the marketplace, was a large flour mill. When times were normal, people brought their wheat there to be ground. The miller took part of this crop as payment for his services, but the families had freshly-ground flour to use.

In this age of plenty, it is hard to understand how special it was just to have white flour. In truth, the roughly-ground brown flour we usually used was almost unpalatable. Every year, as a special treat, my parents went to the mill just before Christmas to purchase white flour to bake special breads and cakes for the holidays. Now, this was no longer possible. We had little money to pay for luxuries and besides, only the Germans could get this flour. In truth, it looked as though we were going to have just the wheat flour that we ground ourselves for the holidays. Our holiday tradition would have to wait for the end of the war. This still was not too bad as it was much better than having nothing at all, which had sadly become the norm.

Irene was still on my mind; I missed her, but for now, it seemed impossible to find her. We had heard that she and my aunt, with whom she had been staying, were being held in the Ukraine. The open war between Germany and Russia seemed to preclude our looking for her.

A few days before Christmas, I happened to glance through the front window and saw a German soldier riding a horse toward our house. As he got closer, I recognized Sergeant Wagner carrying a huge white sack. He stopped his horse, dismounted, came to the back door, and knocked softly.

My parents opened the door and said, "Hello, Sergeant Wagner."

"For you. For Christmas," he said in German as he handed my mother a sack filled with white flour. My parents thanked him with broad smiles and warmth in their eyes. My dad helped mom with the flour; it must have been at least 50 kilos. That much white flour was worth a fortune in those days, and we greatly appreciated the gift.

Sergeant Wagner, we noticed, now wore the insignia of the hated SS on his collar. He did not have this when he lived in our house. He saw us staring at the insignia, and he said in German, "This is nothing," as he pointed to his collar. "It is required that I wear this now. I have a new post. Near here. Did you know that the Americans have now joined in the war?"

"No, I did not," my father answered truthfully with a large smile.

Sergeant Wagner noticed this, but said nothing, "I am leaving again soon, so I guess this is goodbye. Enjoy the flour."

"Where are you going?"

He did not answer, but the implication was clear. He was going to Russia.

"Would you like to stay for dinner, Sergeant?"

"Danke, but no, ma'am. I have to get going."

He placed his hand on my head, mussing my hair a little, and said, "Auf Wiedersehen." After he was gone, my dad was very happy because United States was in the war. "I cannot believe what good news this is. Maybe this war will end soon, and we can all go to America."

"You think it will help?" my mother asked.

"In the long run. But for now it will probably make our position more difficult because we are American citizens."

It seemed to be the way of the war. There was very little

news that was simply good. Even good news was tinged with sadness.

We went to church for the midnight mass and stayed until dawn, celebrating the birthday of Jesus. It was Christmas and my mother cooked a special dinner: duck and that special white bread that she had not made for a long time. It was delicious; for once, we ate our fill.

As I ate, I prayed for Irene again. I wanted her with us—I asked God to help. It seemed as though I had been having a never-ending conversation with God lately. There were so many things that I could not understand. I desperately wanted His help. How can people exist without hope? Why was the Lord permitting these men to kill innocent people so wantonly? What divine purpose could be served by killing defenseless infants? I had so many questions and so few answers that it was extremely frustrating.

Holidays have a way of bringing us a kind of perspective. As it was, I was moderately satisfied with my situation. After all, I was with my family and we were surviving together. That in itself was worth thanking the Lord, for I had known utter aloneness. My family together was its own miracle.

As I went into the barn that evening to take care of my evening chores, I closed my eyes in the stillness of the barn, a stillness very much like that of the manger where Jesus was born. After placing my hands on the side of our cow to keep them warm, I prayed again for Irene. I was so worried about her. While I was grateful that my family was together, her absence was a deep sadness. I prayed long that night, not only for Irene, but for all who had been touched by this dreadful war. But mostly, I prayed for peace.

It was a desolate, cold winter. The temperatures seemed to hover in the teens during the day and then get colder in the night. My father and I used to get up at three o'clock in the morning to go and steal from the Germans. We did not believe that this was wrong; after all in our minds, we were only taking back what the Germans had stolen from us. And while we knew that stealing was wrong, taking back what is rightfully yours is not. At least in our minds. I doubt if the Germans would agree with this line of reasoning. But stealing was simply one of the things we did to survive. There seemed to be a rationale there that certified this activity, and we accepted the rationalization willingly.

As cold as the winter was, we knew that another spring was almost here. We were making plans about what to plant and where to plant it. Mom and Dad were going to plant potatoes and a lot of other vegetables. My father was only waiting for the spring thaw to retrieve the potatoes he had buried for this purpose. But the days dragged on forever.

On the first spring-like day, we let the cow and goat out of the barn. The cow ran around like she was crazy. It was obvious that she did not like being cooped up in the barn. As I watched her cavort on the soggy ground, I remember thinking that humans are not so different.

The cow was very thin. We had not been able to set aside enough hay to keep her fat. But the warmth of spring would soon bring the grasses bursting forth from the ground, and she could eat her fill. I looked forward to this, because then she would begin producing much more milk. We needed the milk for Andrew and to supplement the goat's milk for Sophie. Perhaps there might even be enough to make butter and cheese, delicacies that were absent from our table for most of the winter.

As slowly as the cold days passed, they did indeed pass. During this time, the German army kept moving towards the Russian border. We either saw them going that way or heard them moving in the night. Often, when I heard the machinery moving while I slept, I longed for the quiet nights we used to have. On the road in front of our house, we saw troops moving east and some returning. Those returning had faces set in stone, expressionless and grave. It was as if they were in shock.

We saw many more Russian bombers flying overhead. There was so many of them that they looked like metallic clouds blocking out the sun. They flew more frequently, always having small fighters protecting them. Often, the fighter planes would dive and strafe the countryside. After they left, the sky would be full of smoke, marks left from the anti-aircraft explosions. We just tried to stay out of the way.

My father began plowing and planting. I helped. It was a good time for the two of us. With spring, our hope had been renewed. After plowing, we planted: potatoes, tomatoes, carrots, and a few other crops. With the spring rains falling gently, the grass started to green and grow with abandon. Here and there the greenery was punctuated by wild flowers blooming gayly in the warm air and spring sun. They looked beautiful. The world would have been a beautiful place, but for the war. The war colored everything in shades of black and red.

In Baranowo, as in other towns, there was a mass grave. The one characteristic I will always remember of the Nazis was their penchant for killing. This grave insulted the green countryside and nature tried its best to paint it over with fresh grass. Every day when I took the cow to pasture, I had to pass by this grave. I tried to avert my eyes, but I could not. There was something about the grave that drew me to it. I hated it.

When the grave had been fresh, bones had protruded from the earth. They stood accusing the Germans in broad daylight. Now, these had mostly been covered by the people from the town. The sight of this abomination was deeply offensive. In my mind, I am sure that everyone who brought soil to cover the grave, knew someone buried there. As sad as it was to see the bones of the people poking through, the remains of the tiny children were even more pitiful. I saw these small bones as they poked to the surface seeking the sunlight and serving as prosecutors against the Germans. While these bones had been covered up through the winter, the wind and rain of spring had caused the ground to compact, and they were visible once again.

It was difficult for me to see them as I walked to the pasture. I took it upon myself to cover them, throwing sand on the bones till they disappeared into the earth once more. I could not stay at this place for very long, as the emotions would soon overwhelm me. In the stillness of the countryside, I could swear I heard babies' cries coming from the grave. It taunted me from a place inside myself I could not seem to quell.

I felt I needed to talk to someone about what I was feeling. I had so many different questions about these horrible and unbelievable things that were happening. But the truth is, there was no one to talk to who did not share similar questions. So, we just learned to live with our own nightmares.

I had not seen a smile on anyone's face for a long time. All this nearly made me scream, but I could not. My emotions were so tightly bottled up within me that I could only scream silently—these silent screams were getting louder and louder.

Chapter 17

As it was through most of the war, my family's togetherness was merely temporary. One morning, just after dawn, we heard the door being forced open. The German SS came and dragged my father out of his bed and began beating him; hitting, kicking, striking him with their rifle butts and then, finally, taking him away with them. They offered no explanation of why they were doing this and our pleas remained unanswered.

My mother was devastated; she had three children to take care of and without her husband to help, it would be much more difficult. We all knew this. We heard later that my father had been taken to a labor camp in Stetin. But my grief over having my father taken was soon wrested from me. The next day they came for me as well.

The German police knocked on the door and I was made to work from sunup till sundown digging trenches and gathering peat moss that we called "torf."

The bigger and stronger boys were forced to dig the torf from the swamps. They had to go deep into the water to do this. The water was still terribly cold and they suffered for it. It was dreadfully hard work. If any of these boys slacked in the least way, they were beaten severely or simply killed. When they had brought the torf out of the water, we had to carry it away from the hole and stack it on the ground to dry. This would be used in the German's stoves the next winter.

At the end of every day, I was exhausted. The dampness of the material caused my arms, feet, and legs to become so chapped that they bled. In the afternoon, when the day had warmed sufficiently, the mosquitoes and gnats would attack us. They found my open sores very attractive and swarmed around me. Words fail me when I try to write how gruesome an experience this was. Some things simply have to be experienced to be understood. I believe this is one of them. But I can say, without equivocation, that these days were some of my worst during the war.

It was not too long after my arrival that I began to feel sick. But sickness was not permitted. If you were too sick, you were simply killed. I kept going as best I could. I tried not to show that I was sick, even though I felt as if I had a fever. I focused on the task at hand to keep myself motivated.

We worked everyday without exception. The weather made no difference to the Germans. One hot summer day, several Gendarmes came to where we were working. I was still sick and getting sicker. But I had decided that working sick was preferable to dying, so I continued on. The Gendarmes took two of the oldest boys, boys of just sixteen years, and beat them mercilessly until they passed out from the pain or were knocked unconscious. All the while they were beating these boys, they were screaming in Polish that they were lazy and a bad influence on the rest of us. The show worked, and we redoubled our efforts.

I felt their pain, but I was too sick to get emotional. I just tried to close my mind to what I was seeing and took care of what I could. At the end of the day, I started getting weak and dizzy on the way back from the work area to the barracks. No matter how hard I tried, I kept falling behind the rest. I did not know what to do, because if I could not keep up, there was a very good chance I would be killed.

But be that as it may, I finally succumbed to the sickness and fell first to my knees, then flat on my face in a clump of high grass along the river. The other young men from the camp, I found out later, had covered my body with straw and, most importantly, had not told the Germans that I was gone.

They knew I was sick—they had all seen me vomiting earlier. We were all aware of what happened when one was sick. I am eternally grateful to these unnamed young men. The guards didn't discover me missing until they got to the camp and by that time, they had neither the time nor inclination to search for me. I was left to die.

I slept alongside the river. I was too sick to do anything else. At this point, my memory is a little hazy. I was sleeping in the grass and when I woke up, I was in a bed with a woman offering me some herbal tea.

I took it gratefully and she said, "Here, drink this; it will help with your sickness."

I recognized the lady. She had a house that was on the way from the work camp to the place where we were digging the torf. She was an older woman with a humped back.

She must have told someone about me. Since she was too close to the road, some other people came, took me to their house, and placed me on a bed with a straw mattress.

For the first couple of weeks, I did nothing and do not remember very much. There were no doctors available. These people took care of me as if I had been their own. Homemade remedies mainly: herbs, and cold water wraps for the fever.

I do not know what kind of illness I had, but after about thirty days I felt strong enough to do small things, like fishing in the little lake in that valley or chopping wood. I thanked God for making me well, and I was thinking about moving on. I had become attached to this family that had taken care of me. They had three children, two boys younger than I, and a girl maybe two years older. The lady's name was Kasia, and her husband was Jan.

"Mitchell," Jan said one day, "Your mother knows you are with us."

"Does she? Can I see her?"

"No, not right now. I don't think that would be a good

idea. The Germans are watching your house, as you well know. They think you have escaped from the prison camp, which, of course, you did."

I understood, but I did not like it. I was well now; even my chapped forearms and legs had healed. I felt good and even though I lost a lot of weight, I had gained some of it back. My priorities had changed since my sickness. I wanted to take care of myself better, because I would be ten years old in a few days, the 30th of August.

I had to figure out how to help Mom somehow because winter would be here soon, and I didn't know how she would survive with my little sister and brother. I thought often of my family.

This war dragged on and on. In those quiet days, when I was feeling better but not sure what to do, I thought about myself for a long time. I knew that I had changed. The circumstances of my life had transformed me from a child into some sort of an animal. Sometimes, I was afraid that I would lose my humanity and become an unrepentant beast, like the Nazis.

Beatings, torture, hunger, and constant loneliness can do this to a person. I used to have a daily dialogue with God. I did not even do that anymore. I was simply trying to survive, and if God were not going to help me, I would have to help myself. It was at this time that I lost my faith. But I continued. I was only ten years of age, but my heart was full of anger and darkness. I wanted to bolt away from all of it. I continually screamed inside. I was scared, angry, hungry, and lonely, but my screams were silent.

Even when doing something I enjoyed, this joy was robbed by flashbacks of the things I had seen and felt. If I were fishing and a big fish happened to bite, it did not please me much, because I could see the mass graves in my mind. These are not easily dismissed from one's consciousness.

In the summertime, they smelled terrible. They were disease-ridden and a lot of people became ill, including me. Kasia told me later that she thought I might have had typhoid fever when I was brought to them, but she was not sure. There were so many diseases that made their way through the population that it could have been any number of them.

The thought that I should not be complaining came to me as well. I was temporarily free, but what about those people in the Treblinka camp? We had heard from someone who had escaped from there that they were killing thousands people a week—children and adults. The rumor was that they were trying to exterminate the Jewish race. But their murderous activities were not limited to Jews; they were killing anyone who was not of the Aryan race. This included Poles and other groups. If I had not witnessed the brutality, I would have dismissed these statements as exaggerations. Simply, there is no way to exaggerate the evil of the Nazis.

To survive, I began developing a strange sense of humor. To laugh at such things does not make sense, but it helped to suppress my silent screams. From my perspective as an adult, developing this way of looking at things was necessary for my survival. It was a strategy for coping, but at the time, I did not understand this. I thought I was losing my mind.

When Placek, the German police commandant, beat me with the horsewhip, I remember looking at him and laughing on the inside. I looked at his ugly, frustrated face, the jowls of which shook when he screamed, and my heart smiled. He was having a hard time with me; that pleased me. Every time he hit me, this deep-felt smile eased the blow. I looked at him through the pain and thought, "Look at that fat German. How ridiculous and stupid he looks!" His screaming voice faded until it became a meaningless echo. This was strange, but it did help me to transcend the ruthlessness of the moment, and to survive.

In spite of this, I feared that I had lost hope. There were times when I could not control my emotions; the tears ran down my face. I would lose control and sob helplessly like a baby. I heard myself raging at God, "Please either help me or take me." It eased my pain somewhat, but it did not quell the silent screams.

Chapter 18

With the passing of time and seasons, it was now November. It had been more than three years since the beginning of this nightmare war. I decided that I missed my mother enough to chance a visit. I knew this was dangerous, but I also knew that I longed for my home.

I left the family I had been staying with and began my journey alone. I thanked Kasia and Jan and their family as best I could. I knew that they had saved my life, and I was grateful. Without their help the disease I was suffering from would have killed me. We all shed tears, but it was time I moved on. It was not easy leaving, but it would have been harder to stay.

That is one of my chief remembrances of the war: being alone. Even in Kasia and Jan's house, I was still an outsider. I was only ten, but I had been alone more than is normal for any young boy. And while they did their best to make me feel welcome, I still missed my home and my family.

I walked alone through the still forest heading for Baranowo. It was not a difficult trip. The weather had turned, and it was almost pleasant walking. Occasional sounds of the war invaded the stillness of the deep woods, silencing the ambient sounds. With each distant rumble of the guns, the birds fell quiet, and the squirrels stopped their ever-restless quest for nourishment. Only my footsteps echoed loudly in the remaining silence.

When I encountered the main road leading to Baranowo, I saw the German army still on the move. The men and equipment continued to make a steady processional to the east. In counterpoint, there was a steady stream of men returning from the Eastern Front. Their faces were no longer full of bravado. They looked defeated as they hobbled along with a sense of brokenness about them. It was easy to see that many of them were grievously wounded. I looked on, safe in my hiding place as they passed. Retreating to the forest, I continued heading for my home.

When I reached the outer perimeters of town, I skirted the city by keeping to the deep pine woods that surrounded the area. I knew that I would have to wait until dark before going home. I sincerely hoped the moon would not be bright enough to make the Germans aware of my presence.

I was afraid. Kasia and Jan had told me that the Nazis in Baranowo were forming hunting parties to look for any Polish young man who was away from their home at night and might be going to join the Underground. When they found one, they would shoot him and place his body on the school's porch to discourage any others who might think of leaving their homes to fight against them. The Germans were very good at raising terror among the people they conquered.

Though I was younger than most of the young men whom they were hunting, this prospect still frightened me. I did not think that they would shoot a boy as young as me, but in the darkness they could make a mistake. I did not want to die, and I certainly did not want to be put on display as a trophy by the bloodthirsty Nazis. I was extremely careful as I crossed the fields that led into town.

Rather than go straight to my house, I decided to stop by my aunt's and see what was happening. The night was cold and my breath hung in the air as I walked toward their house by the cemetery and the church. I thought I would try to find out if it was safe, and this house was a lot closer to me than ours. When I neared the house, I saw a small crack of light escaping from the edge of the window. The people of the town were under orders to cover the windows with blankets or the Nazis would throw a grenade through the window.

I crept closer and picked up a very small rock. Taking careful aim, I threw it at the window. I knew that the Germans were assigning soldiers to private houses as this had happened to my family with Sergeant Wagner. I did not want to try to enter the house if it is was not safe for my aunt's family or me.

I watched the light dim through the crack. My heart was beating rapidly and my breath came quickly. Then I saw a woman come out. It was my Aunt Helen. I moved from the shadows as she came closer. She recognized me with a start and said, "Mitchell, so good to see you. Come in, come in."

She welcomed me into her arms and hugged me warmly. "We were so concerned about you. Are you okay? We heard that you had been sick."

"I am doing okay now. I was sick, but I got better. Is my mom okay?" I asked.

"Yes, I guess she is. Your father is not with her now though."

"Where is he? Do the Nazis still have him?"

"Yes, I guess they do. He had been home with your mom for a while, but there has been some trouble in town and they have arrested a bunch of men."

My uncle, who was throwing handfuls of pine needles into the stove, began coughing violently. My aunt rushed to him with a pan and he coughed up blood. He had been held in a Russian prison for a long time and although he had escaped, his health was poor.

"Aunt Helen, I want to go home now. Do you think it is safe?"

"It should be. They have not been looking for you for some time now, and the police and SS people have nearly all been changed."

"Thanks for welcoming me; it's nice to see you again."

"But aren't you going to stay for something to eat?"

The question hung in the air. In truth, I had not had anything to eat for a long time and I was very hungry. But I also wanted to see my family. "No, I have to get going, but thank you," I said as I moved out of the small house.

When I got close to home, my mom was outside talking to a neighbor woman. They watched me approach cautiously. When she heard my voice, my mom started running towards me with my neighbor close behind her. I ran toward her, as well. As we were running, I heard her scream for joy, a scream she stifled almost immediately lest she be discovered.

When she was close to me, she grabbed me and started kissing me. "Oh, Mitch, I'm so happy to see you." I felt the wet tears running down her face as she started sobbing. My neighbor also hugged me. While I was being welcomed by the women, I felt there was something wrong.

My neighbor went back to her house and my mom welcomed me inside. I ran to Andrew and Sophie and hugged and kissed them both. It felt so good to be home.

"Have you seen Dad, Mom? I heard he is in jail in town here."

"That's true," she sobbed.

"What is wrong?"

"Your father had just gotten home—a couple of days is all—when he was arrested with 29 other men from town. The Germans are interrogating and torturing them because an SS man was killed. The commandant announced that if the man who shot the Nazi is not found in seven days, the thirty men who are in jail will be hanged in front of the church."

I did not know what to say. I held her close and tried to whisper reassuring words, but neither of us believed them. My time of happiness was short-lived once more.

My brother Andrew came over to us as if he sensed something was wrong, and we all hugged. My sister started to cry, so I reached with my foot and rocked her crib gently.

My mother looked terrible. Her tears had dried but her face remained puffy and her eyes were swollen. "You must be hungry, Mitchell. Would you like some potato soup? I can make you some and maybe there will be enough so that you can bring some to your father in the morning."

I did not answer; I did not need to. Knowing I was hungry, she was soon bustling around the kitchen making a small pot of soup. "Mitchell, there is a window at the back of the jail. I think that you can try to get some soup to your father through it."

"Yes, Mom, I know about the window."

After I ate, we sat together long into the night visiting. It felt so good to have someone break my loneliness. "When you got sick, the SS men came looking for you here."

"What did you say?"

"I did not know anything, so what could I say? This did not seem to stop them from beating me to make sure I was telling the truth."

"They beat you! Because of me?"

"Yes. But don't blame yourself. The Nazis like to beat people, I think."

"Oh, Mom. I am so sorry," I said as I moved from my seat and hugged her tightly. "I didn't want you to suffer. I just didn't know what to do."

"You did the right thing," she said.

"Do you think the police will bother me tomorrow?"

"No, most of them are new and they seem preoccupied. The important thing is to remember that they have promised to hang your father in five days." She then burst into tears once again.

Finally, I was exhausted and said, "Mom, I'd like to go to bed. I'm tired."

"Certainly, Mitchell."

I lay down on a straw mattress. Before I fell asleep, I thought how right it felt to be with my family again, even though some of them weren't here. I had missed my little brother and sister. For this fleeting, precious moment I savored being under our roof with them, and with Mom, of course. As for Dad, I hoped that I would see him tomorrow morning and learn how he was going to get out of this situation.

Chapter 19

That night, I think I slept as well as I ever had. While I was concerned for my father, seeing my family again after such a long time had eased my mind considerably. It seemed that as soon as my head touched the pillow, I was gone and did not stir again until my sister's cry woke me.

I wandered from my room and saw my mom busily working in the kitchen. Mom had baked fresh bread; the house still smelled of it and made my mouth water. She had taken a large piece and rolled it in a rag for me to take to the jail and my father. The soup from last night was warming on the stove and she said, "Sit and have some soup and bread. You must be hungry."

I was, and I ate the food gratefully. As I sat in the warm kitchen, I looked out of the window at the barn and wondered if Moshe's family had made it safely to England. My thoughts were disturbed by my mom saying, "Here, I want you to bring this soup and bread to your father. Better get going soon though; it is nearly noon."

As I walked out of the door holding the bread and soup, I was excited about seeing my father, even under these circumstances. It had been such a long time. I had some concern as I walked and had butterflies in my stomach. I tried to appear as inconspicuous as possible. I had hidden the bread in my coat and held the soup to my side.

My concern rose from the fact that I knew that I was not entirely safe. There was the possibility that German sympathizers would tell the Nazis that I had escaped from the work camp. Another of the difficulties of this situation was not knowing whom to trust. Now, from my adult perspective, I think I understand. When everything you have ever known is called into question, a person will do whatever they can to survive. At the time, I did not feel this way, but time has a way of making these thoughts more clear.

I knew the camp where we mined the torf was now only a memory. The torf operation had been closed. I also knew that in its place, they had built many others. While they could not return me to the same work camp, this did not ease my situation appreciably. There were other camps that might be even worse than the hell-hole I had escaped.

The morning was crisp and cold; the dusting of snow on the ground crunched beneath my feet. I bundled myself up as much as I could and wore a hat pulled down over my ears. The hat was not so much for the cold as it was to disguise my appearance. My mother had told me that prior to this incident, the Germans had posted a directive that if a German national were killed, fifty men would die in his place.

However, in the small town of Baranowo, there were no longer fifty men available to kill. The able-bodied men had all been shipped to either labor camps or concentration camps at Auschwitz, Treblinka, or Dachau. Those who had managed to avoid this fate were hiding in the forests surrounding the town. Some of these men were with the Underground, while some were just hiding. I guess that is the reason they took my father and the others. While there were not fifty men, it did not seem to change the danger to my father and the others.

I saw the Gmina, or city hall, looming before me. In a simpler time, it was a source of community pride. Now, it was the place the Germans had taken for their own—like Poland. When I got closer, I went around in back to the alley.

I noticed that I could squeeze in between an old wooden rotten fence, which led into the yard and the back of the jail. At the rear of the facility were two very small windows with bars over them. We had never had much crime in my city, before the Germans, so the cells in the jail were not adequate for the needs of this many people. The Germans did not care.

As I neared, I saw that the lower window would have been easier for me, but the one that was elevated was abutting the wooden fence and would offer some cover. I slipped through the rotting fence and climbed to the window and softly called for my father. As I waited for a response, I noticed that the window was broken out and there was a terrible smell emanating in the steam from the place. It smelled of human feces and suffering, a fetid smell I have never managed to cleanse from my mind since I first encountered it at the Russian prison.

My father moved to the window, reached his hand through and grasped mine tightly. "Mitchell, you are here!"

"I am! I got home last night. Mom made you some food. Here," I said as I handed him the soup and bread. He took them gratefully and asked, "How are your mom and the kids?"

"They are fine, but missing you."

My father was much thinner now than I remembered. A cloud passed over his face as he answered, "I know. I miss them too. I am happy to see you. I just wish I weren't here."

"I know," I replied.

When I looked at him again, tears streaked down his face cleaning the dirt and leaving small lines. I felt terrible. My father and I had always been close. It was hard seeing him in this precarious situation. I felt my own tears beginning.

"Mitchell, there are only five days left before they hang us."

"I know. What are you going to do?"

There was no answer. What was he supposed to say? I looked a little closer and noticed that his face was horribly bruised. "Are you okay?" I asked.

"I am okay. I am more concerned about your mother,

Andrew, and Sophie. And you, of course," he added

"We are surviving."

I saw movement in the city hall and thought it best that I leave. "Dad, I have to go. Someone is coming."

"I understand. Can you come back?"

"Yes, I will be back later. Take care."

When I jumped off the fence, my dad's question trailed after me: "Have you heard any news of Irene?'

"No. Not yet. I hope soon." I said it knowing that I was merely trying to ease his mind. I ran off through the hole in the fence and started for home.

I went into the woods to make my way back home. Although our house was on the main street, I did not want to use it for fear of discovery. When I arrived, my mom was breast-feeding Sophie, but she stopped immediately. "How is your father?"

"He is okay. I know he liked the food. I don't think they are feeding them very well."

My mother was very nervous. She paced around the kitchen while she asked me question after question. Some of these were easily answered, some there simply was no answer for, and she knew it.

Before long, she covered her face with her hands and began sobbing softly. She moved to her chair and sat. I crossed the room and tried my best to comfort her. I hugged her tightly and whispered, "Everything will work out. You will see." Even though I said the words, I was less than certain and felt the burden of my own doubt and helplessness.

Our circumstances were difficult. The winter was here, and we had little food. We did not even have the wood pile replenished. There was little to burn to keep the winter cold away. There were some things that I could do, but the fact was that in order to survive, we needed the help of my father.

I was only a boy; he was a man.

As I held my mother and tried to comfort her that day, I hoped the Russians would bomb Baranowo. At least that would ease my parents' pain and it might afford my father a chance to escape. In truth, I did not see how he was going to survive this.

As my mother recovered a little composure, I decided to go and see if could find some food. I left home and headed to where the German mess was located. I walked with my small pot in my hands and joined the other boys waiting around for a handout.

I could tell that these men had been at the Russian front. Those who had been there had a look about them. Their cruelty was mollified.

The other boys waiting there did not talk. Instead, we just watched with hungry eyes. This was a normal part of life in occupied Poland. Sometimes an SS guard would come and chase the local boys away. But not always. On this day, I waited patiently.

I saw two soldiers who must have been friends. I could tell by the easy way they spoke to each other. I saw them as they watched me. Saying something in German, they left their seats and took their mess kits to the serving line. When they returned, they motioned me over.

Taking their kits, they motioned for my bucket. I gave it to them, and they emptied their food into it. When they handed it back to me, I thanked them. I took the small pot in both hands and felt the warmth through the metal. My mouth watered, but I took the stew and ran home.

I was excited and proud. When I got to my home, I handed the pot to my mom. I could tell she was pleased, too. She chopped the meat and gave some to Andrew. She took some for herself and gave me a portion as well. She left some for my father.

Chapter 20

The stew from the German soldiers was excellent, and we savored it. Meat had gone the way of most luxuries in the war. We seldom had enough money to afford it, and if we had the money, it was simply not available. Most of the food went to the military first. When they were satisfied, remnants might be available to the civilian population. They were seldom satisfied.

When I awoke the next morning, I played with Andrew for a while and talked with my mom. Sophie's cries had pierced the stillness of the morning, but she was a baby, and I understood. Mom apologized, but I knew that it was normal. Normal was something I both craved and appreciated. Her cries were so much superior to being awakened with a, "Heil Hitler!" bellowing in my ear. No, these baby sounds were welcome.

It would not do to go to the jail too early. If I went early, the police would be more involved with their prisoners. Typically, at the beginning of their shifts, they were more active than they were in the middle. I knew this, so I waited until about nine o'clock. Mom gave me the stew that was left from last night with a piece of bread and a bit of goat's milk in a bottle.

Again, I took the long way, and I tried to keep away from the main streets. I saw some people I knew, but they didn't recognize me in my disguise. I just appeared as another young boy.

Polish towns, like those nearly everywhere, are organized around a central square. In the case of Baranowo, this was a circle. There was an open space in the center with the buildings situated around it. The jail was a cement building located on the edge of the town's circle and housed two large cells. Each cell had a window; the one where my father was located was the cell with the high window. This remained a problem. In order to reach this window, I had to reach with my left hand fully extended, and my dad had to do the same. Because of this, I knew that I would have to climb that fence again.

However, when I climbed the fence, I was completely visible from the city hall building. There was a man there—Orzel—an informer. Orzel had a despicable reputation in town. He was called a dog by the people. If calling him names made him feel less than good, we never knew it. Instead, he had decided to throw his lot with the Germans and would do whatever was necessary to endear himself to them.

Orzel carried a Luger and prided himself on his marksmanship. Many people had suffered by his hand. I was more afraid of him than the German police.

There were some old men and women talking near the jail, and I mingled among them. I overheard them say that the police just brought one man back from interrogation and had taken another. I hoped that it wasn't my father.

I moved to the back of the jail and watched as a man left the rear of the building carrying two buckets full of human waste. He took these and dumped them into the outside toilets. I waited.

Another lesson the war had taught me was patience. It would not be very smart to do anything to draw attention to myself, so I waited and watched. Apparently, the Germans were taking one man at a time out and interrogating him. I say interrogate, but torture would be a better word. The victim's screams ripped the silence of the Polish morning. It seemed that they were taking one man every half hour or so. I say this because it was not always thirty minutes. Sometimes, it was shorter, and other times much longer. It depended on how long it was before the man passed out from the pain and ended their interrogation. My own pain from being tortured in that building returned, and I shuddered.

I had to be really careful when I went to see my dad. I did not want to cause him any more pain. He had told me in our brief visit yesterday that they had taken him twice already. He said that most did not survive beyond the third or fourth interrogation.

I moved cautiously and slid between the boards of the rotten fence again. This had to be done quickly to escape discovery. I put the food I had brought on top of the fence post and climbed on top. My dad was already watching for me by the window. I handed him the food, and he asked, "How is everyone at home?"

"We are fine. But very worried about you."

"I know. I am worried about you as well. Tell mom I love her, also your brother and sister."

My father, who was looking at the window of the city hall, saw a man's body from the waist up running back and forth. When the man in the city hall opened the window, my father said, "Look out, Mitchell, jump!"

I jumped down from the fence and ran. I still took the back way home. I did not know what was going to happen, so I felt great relief when I made it home.

When I got there, my mom was making some watery soup with potatoes and a few beans. I hugged her tightly. I was still scared, and my heart was pounding furiously as I held onto her. "Dad sends his love to us." She looked as if her thoughts were a million miles away. She was terrified of losing Dad, and so was I.

All that day I tried to think of a way out of this situation for my father. In my misery, I even thought of trying to leave a light on in the yard of the jail. At least if the Russians bombed it, it would end the men's misery. But the weather had not cooperated. It had been overcast for the last few days, and the Russian planes were not flying.

On the fifth day after I arrived home, I got up early with Mom. My little sister's crying woke us up again. Mom sat down in the homemade chair with Sophie in her arms and breast-fed her; she stopped crying. Mom had to drink some milk every day in order to have some milk for little Sophie. Most of the time she drank goat's milk and very little of that. Milk was a precious commodity and could be traded with the Germans for oil for the lamp or a bit of flour, but there was seldom any left.

That morning remains emblazoned in my mind. My mother had cooked some watery soup and potato pancakes. They tasted good, but we both knew that this was the final day, and the dawn of the next day would bring the mass hangings the Germans had promised. I tried not to think about it, but the vision of the men hanging was clear in my mind.

I took the food she had prepared and headed for town. The snow was falling, but it was a light dusting with little accumulation. Instead it swirled in the wind and colored the world white. I ran. I was anxious to see my dad. In truth, I had given up hope of his being freed. This might be the last time I could see him. It was unthinkable.

When I got to the city hall yard, I carefully looked around and with caution moved the boards on the fence so I could get through the hole. Everything looked unusually quiet, and when I got closer, I could again smell the people through the broken window; I jumped on the fence, balancing myself. I gave my dad the food. While I was passing him the food, I held on to the corner of the building with my right hand.

My dad took the food, and suddenly yelled,"Mitch, look out!" He was looking past me in the direction of the city hall window. When I turned my head to look, the man in window shot.

I felt the bullet hit me in the head, and I fell to the ground. I lay there and tried to think. I did not appear to be badly hurt, so I got up and started running. As I was running to the fence, the man shot two more times. He missed. I got through the fence and ran toward home. It hurt. I did not know what was going to happen, so I simply ran as fast as my legs would carry me—as if, by running, I could escape the bullet that had already found me, its target.

I was about halfway home when I felt a wetness on my face. I touched it and looked—blood. Blood was streaming from the top of my head. I was getting a little dizzy.

When I got home, I opened the door and entered. "Mom, I've been shot!" I said. My mom had a neighbor lady visiting, and they both jumped up and ran toward me. I do not remember a lot about what happened after that. I know the neighbor's husband was among those thirty men in the jail, and she had become a frequent visitor.

The two women led me to a chair and carefully took off my bloody hat and scarf. I remember the worried look on my mom's face as she washed my head with water. When she was done, she took her scissors and cut my hair around the wound. When the hair was short enough, she took my dad's straight razor and shaved around the area. After cleaning the area again, she made a poultice of leaves and wrapped it in a white towel she had cut up. She tied this around my chin holding it in place and led me to my bed.

Both women helped me to lie down. I wanted to sleep, but my mom would not let me. Instead, she talked soothingly to me. She kept me awake the rest of that day and most of the night. When it was near morning, I was permitted to go to sleep, and it felt wonderful.

While I was sleeping, the vision of Orzel, laughing as he pulled the trigger on his Luger, invaded my mind.

When I woke the next morning, who should I see but my father.

"Dad! What are you doing here?"

"I've been released. They found the man who killed the SS man, so they simply let us go."

"Was it one of the men with you?"

"No, it was someone else. A man hung himself, but he left a note confessing to killing the man. Mitchell, it is wonderful to see you! I'm sorry you got shot; I was worried about how you were going to make it home. Your mom looked at the wound and says you are going to be fine. It appears you are still a survivor."

It was indeed a superficial wound, though it gave me an awful headache. I still get the headaches often. There were no doctors around, so my mom tried to end my headaches with all kinds of home remedies. None of them worked, but I did not tell her.

Chapter 21

Having my father with us, after his time in the jail, probably saved our lives. The war has a lot of ways of killing people. Whether it is the Germans, the bombs, or your own people, there are myriad ways to die. One of the most effective agents of death is starvation. In our land of plenty, it is hard to imagine slowly wasting away and having energy sapped from your body until ultimately you are too tired to do anything. I can testify that this happens. One gets so weary physically and so disheartened psychologically, it is hard to even imagine being satisfied. Starvation was our constant companion, and every day we fought against it.

For the next month my dad did his best to prepare us for winter. He moved in hay for the cow and the two goats and such food for us as he could find, which was not a lot. At this time, I was not able to help him very much because I was still recovering. Although the injury from Orzel's gun was not life-threatening, it still was a grievous wound; it caused me to become sick and dizzy whenever I tried to do too much. However, the wound was healing, and I thanked God for the gift of life he had granted me. Sometimes, I would lie awake at night and gratefully touch the crease in my head and think of how lucky I was to still be here.

The late fall became a cold winter. We were barely surviving; there was hardly enough to eat and no way to get any more. Christmas came anyway. My mother, who had been hoarding some flour, made fresh bread and cookies. These cookies had to be made without the proper ingredients, and they were simply awful. What should have been a joyous occasion, was not.

The cookies were cut into squares before she put them in the oven. In the oven they turned into these dreadful hard balls. When she gave one to me, I tried to bite it. When I could not, I threw it to my brother Andrew. It fell to the floor with a thud. She looked at me with her eyes blazing, "Mitchell, we are so short on food. God gave us this to eat, not to throw on the ground. I don't want you to ever do this again! Do you understand?"

I guess I didn't. I was at that age when certain knowledge transcends reason, and I replied with a curse. She moved across the room and taking her open hand, struck me. "Don't ever say that word again."

The fire in her eyes convinced me that I should not. When she hit me, it hurt. She was a large woman, and her blow nearly lifted me off my feet. When a mother strikes her child, the blow is deeper than flesh. It was as if she were rebuking my existence. I felt ashamed because I realized how wrong I had been. She was right, and I knew it.

In January, 1943, the weather was bitter cold with heavy snows. When my dad and I went out at night to steal food, I could hardly keep up with him because of the depth of the snow. His legs were longer and able to move more easily. I struggled through the snow, but I did keep up. The snow made our thievery much more difficult. When you are stealing, it is always best not to get caught. The snow made this difficult. It is fairly obvious, with the new snow on the ground, where the thief is going. If we had stuck to the woods, as we used to, I am certain that they could use their dogs and eyes to trace us to our house.

To solve this problem, it was necessary that we use the main road. This amplified the danger considerably, and I knew it. The German army, some tramping to Russia and an equal number coming home made the road hard and compacted the snow, so our footprints were lost with countless others. We moved to the side and watched the road carefully. It would not do to be out on the road so late at night. The implication would be clear, and since, as ordinary citizens without a country we had so few rights, it is likely we would either be arrested or simply shot on the spot.

Watching for the Germans, we used the road until we were near the place where we were going to try to steal something; then we left the main road to slip in. Taking what we could, we made our way back to the road for the trip home. The snow only multiplied the risk of our being discovered.

The stillness of the winter was hardly disturbed. The snow hushed our pain, and we simply tried our best to survive. The nearly constant motion of the Germans on the road was interrupted periodically by the cold silence. It was disquieting to try and survive. I helped my father keep the stove warm, but we hardly had food to eat.

On bright and sunny days, the bombers appeared in the sky searching for the Germans. Most days, however, were overcast, and this made it too difficult for the bombers to find a target. It was as if the world were taking a deep breath.

It gave me a lot of time to think and hope and dream. My dreams at this age were of getting away from this awful war. I hated it, and I wanted something better for both myself and my family. I knew this was impossible, but I could not help dreaming. When you stop dreaming, you might as well die.

My young life was perpetually overshadowed by our terrible hunger and this dreadful war. My father and I talked for long hours. He told me about America and what it would be like when we got there. I knew he was trying to give me hope, and I appreciated it. But I also knew that our path to the United States was blocked by so many obstacles, it seemed impossible.

He tried to comfort me. I remember him telling me that he was also afraid and that being scared was normal. "Mitchell, when you are afraid or if you have a problem, it is important to share. God gave us each other to help."

"I know. But the war..." my words dissolved in the stillness.

Being a child of God was hard when it seemed the devil was winning all around us. But my father had a great faith, and he tried to impart this faith to me. He seemed to have a sixth sense that told him when my heart was full of darkness. Comforting me, he would say, "Mitchell, you know the world is a better place because you are here. I know it is difficult to imagine, but the world will be better some day, and you will look back on these days and marvel that you were so strong."

My mother was a good woman. There was never a doubt that she loved me and my family very much. But I also knew that she was being overtaxed by our circumstances. Since it was up to her to feed us, I know that this troubled her. It is hard to make food out of nothing and even harder to do it day after day. Besides, with Sophie and Andrew needing supervision most of the time, her capacity to cope was being overwhelmed. I was expected to help, and I did so, willingly.

I still talked to the Lord every day. My voice, weak and shaking because I was starving, would sound in the stillness. The questions I asked mostly remained unanswered. The central question was always, "Why?" I did not understand how people could be so dreadful to each other. How can they kill? How can they revel in their evil? I did not understand.

The hunger of that winter is still with me to this day. I needed food as I was growing, but there was none. Instead of growing and becoming stronger, I continued to lose weight, as my family did. Being emaciated and having no reserves made the task of surviving that much more insurmountable.

I still went to the German army kitchen sometimes, but

not as often as before. The truth was that the soldiers shared little with us poor, starving children. And if they showed any compassion, the SS were quick to punish them severely for helping to alleviate our suffering.

I would stand there, with the other starving boys, and wait for them to throw a crust of bread. It was so demeaning and dehumanizing. I felt like a dog begging by the side of the table.

All that winter I watched the road in front of our house. Often I saw the German troops coming back from the Russian front. They appeared to be beaten and disillusioned. We saw ambulances full of soldiers. Most of these were suffering from frostbite and gangrene. Even from the side of the road, I could smell them. It smelled like defeat.

While seeing the Germans suffer might have brought me pleasure, it did not. Instead, it just exacerbated our misery. I hoped they would lose and go away, but mostly I hoped for the end of this ruthless war that takes so much and gives only suffering for all its cost.

I knew they were losing. It was obvious. The look in their eyes as they passed in front of me was enough to convince me of this. They appeared lifeless, nothing more than shells. Their eyes were dead, as all of ours were. With the cold, their vehicles would not start. The roads were nearly impassible. The strategies that had helped them conquer Europe were not working well in the frozen wasteland of Russia. We had also heard that the Germans were amazed at the fighting ability of the Russian soldiers. They assumed, wrongly, that the soldiers would just capitulate. The Russians fought with incredible ferocity.

If the German soldiers appeared nothing more than empty shells, I was doing even worse. Nearly everything that was me was gone: My smile. My hope. My dreams. Instead, what was left was a questing creature seeking only enough to eat.

Dreams at this time became nothing more than enough to eat and a bit of warmth to sleep. My sense of humor and my laughter were completely depleted. Life was ceasing to have meaning anymore. Why survive until tomorrow, when tomorrow just brings more suffering? The question was asked, but never answered. I did not choose to die, I guess. I could have. It would have been easy. Dying is always easy; it is living that is hard.

Still, I was grateful to God for most of my family being together at this time, although I missed Irene terribly. I had endless conversations with God about her. I was not all that patient in my asking, but it did little good. I still had flashes of optimism, but these were soon eroded by the sadness, misery, despair, and hunger. Helplessness of the soul is a desolate, terrible thing.

Chapter 22

One day my dad wanted me to go with him to the train station at Jastrzabka. With the mention of the name and the location, the thought of the atrocities I had witnessed there came to mind. A cloud of sorrow passed in my mind. The vision of that mother and baby being murdered had become a part of my existence. It was a memory I had unsuccessfully tried to banish.

"Mitchell, I have heard that some people are coming in from the East. And one man has just escaped the Russian prison system. One of them might know something about your sister Irene."

I never knew how my father came by his information, but usually it was at least partially true. Truth in the time of war is not all that common. I knew that any news of our family would be welcome. I say any news, because without information the mind tends to delve into the darker places of our existence.

With some trepidation, I followed my father down the forest path toward the station. It was not a long distance. And, after we had walked a kilometer, a farmer's wagon passed us. The farmer said, "If you would like a ride, jump in." We accepted willingly. Riding in a wagon made us less suspect than we would be simply walking. This was a blessing.

He took us to Jastrzabka. When he saw the train pull into the station, he stopped. His horse was becoming skittish from the train's noise, and he had to get down from the wagon to calm the animal. He took the horse by the reins and led the wagon behind a building. Removing the animal from the scene helped, and the horse soon settled down and only emitted an occasional whinny.

As the train came to a stop, I noticed that it contained boxcars full of men. I could see their faces through the slats. "Russian prisoners," my father said as we watched.

As we observed this pastiche of degradation, a man's head was thrown from the train followed by some bones. The bones were white and had little flesh remaining. "Cannibalism!" my father spat.

I looked to him for direction; he had none to give. As I watched, I thought another part of him died in that instant. To see such depravity was as shocking as anything I can imagine. I was sickened and turned my head away.

As I nestled into my father's coat, the remembrance of the things that I had witnessed flashed in my mind. What was it about this station that was so evil? It was as if this were a place where the evil we knew existed, thrived and showed itself proudly. So many horrific things had happened here.

But I knew that terrible things were happening everywhere. Whatever humanity we possessed was being brazenly stolen from us. Yet, knowing this did not ease the pain of the man's head being tossed out as if it were of no more importance than the wrapper on some food that was gone.

I knew it was not just this place, but I could not convince myself of this. For when I came here, I saw the worst of men. When I think of this evil, it has an effect on me. My body goes numb, and my brain retreats deep into some other pocket of existence. I know why. I just don't know what to do about it. As I clung to my father's coat that day trying to erase this abomination, he said, "Let's go, son." He took my arm and pulled me away.

We went over a small hill and into the great forest of pine trees. There were a few houses alongthe forest's edge, and we walked by them. We came to a house constructed of logs, and my father said, "This is it."

As we walked from the forest to the house, we were anxious. The truth was that we wanted news so badly. I think I was even shaking a little when my father knocked at the door.

A man answered. He was neither old nor young, but he had been grievously wounded. One arm was gone and the entire left side of his body looked as though it had been damaged with shrapnel.

"I am Joseph Garwolinski, and this is my son Mitch. I have heard that you may have some information about my family."

"Please come in, Mr. Garwolinski," he said in a gentle voice. "Please sit down and have some hot kasza."

"Thank you very much; we would like that," my father answered as he ushered me in the door. Kasza is a kind of grain soup. It is not terrible to eat and is nutritious. On this cold day, the warmth of the soup would make it taste even better.

"My name is Bolek," the man said as he extended his one good arm. My dad shook his hand and thanked him again. They moved to the living room area and sat.

They had a son. He was a little older than I. He asked, "Would you like to play chess?"

"Yes, I would like that as long as you don't beat me—too badly."

We both smiled at the small joke, and that felt good. After the scene of depravity I had just witnessed, sitting and playing a game with another boy helped.

I did not actually want to play the game. Instead, I wanted to listen to the conversation that my father and his father were having. While my father was anxious for news, so was I.

The boy's name was Bolek as well. I tried to play, but my attention kept straining to hear the information that the man was telling my father. "...in this prison. In the Ukraine, the guards were raping the women. The Germans let them...I have not heard of your wife's sister and your daughter...I did not know everyone..."

The words came to me and caused me much pain. How could they hurt my aunt and my sister? My thoughts retreated further, and I asked God in that still small voice, the one that comes from deep within our existence, how he could allow this to happen. He did not answer.

Bolek's wife interrupted everyone, "The soup is hot. Come and eat."

We left our positions and headed to the kitchen table and sat. My soup was served in a small bowl with a piece of homemade bread. My father got a bigger bowl and two slices of bread. He gave me one of the slices of bread. He knew I was hungry.

The soup was tasty and hot, and it made me feel better, warmer at least. After I slurped the soup and ate the bread, I felt a great sadness descending on me again. Now, the idea of my sister being abused in a Ukrainian prison camp would not leave me. I was glad that I did not hear that my sister and aunt were there. But this did little to ease the pain because someone's sister and aunt were the ones being abused.

After we finished, the boy and I resumed our game. I was trying to play, but I was also trying to listen to the news that Bolek was giving my father. My dad kept asking questions about different labor camps where my sister Irene and my aunt could be. "I don't know, Joseph. They could be anywhere. Dachau or Treblinka are bigger, but they could be anywhere. They could even be behind the Eastern Front. I just don't know."

"I know you don't, Bolek, but thank you for listening and telling me what you know. I appreciate it."

Finally, my father rose. I took his signal and said goodbye to the boy. I was glad to leave. I wanted to be home. "Joseph, I watch the trains go by everyday. Most of them are filled with either Jews, or Polish and Russian prisoners. I think these men are cannibalizing each other." If Bolek hoped to shock us, he failed. My father looked him straight in the eye and said, "That is true. We just witnessed it."

We took a different way through the forest, which wasn't too padded down from the traffic. The snow was deeper, and walking was difficult. I was tired from the labor of moving through the mounds, but I continued trudging alongside my father.

On the way home we didn't talk very much. I could see the disappointment on Dad's face and, more importantly, in his eyes. They clearly showed pain and worry. It seemed that everyday brought a new atrocity, and we were deeply hurt. Not as individuals, but as a people. It is terrible to comprehend the depths of degradation that encompasses people. I felt the same disappointment of not hearing about my sister and my aunt. I also felt an inner helplessness when I realized that they might be tortured or raped. The visions that presented themselves were too terrible to express in words.

My father, as if sensing my thoughts, took my hand in his. This had the effect of banishing these dark thoughts, at least temporarily. I reached into my pocket for a chunk of bread that the woman gave me just before we left the house, and I asked, "Do you want some of this bread, Dad?"

"No, you go ahead and eat it."

I ate the bread as we walked. The silence of the winter forest was overwhelming. It was as if disturbing this silence would be wrong, so we just walked.

At any other time he would have been trying to teach me math and telling me stories. My father loved to relate stories that he had read. I mostly enjoyed listening to him. The only time I did not was when he was going on and on about the importance of reading. I tried to study and read a lot, but it was difficult to study when I was both hungry and cold.

When we got home, it was getting dark already. My mom was lighting the naphtha lamp as we were entering the house. The wind from the door put out the flame since it wasn't covered yet with the glass cover. We walked in; my dad kissed my mom and little Sophie. Andrew ran to my dad, and my dad hugged him; then my dad lit the lamp.

Mom had some potato pancakes for supper with a little milk. I love potato pancakes the way Mom made them, except most of the time there was no oil to fry them in. This time there was enough oil, and they were delicious. Being home helped ease the dark thoughts, and I relished the distraction eating provided.

Chapter 23

The trip we had just completed had taken its toll. Again, like so many other images had done, the vision of the scene of horror at the train station would not leave me alone. It hovered at the edge of my consciousness, waiting to catch me unawares. When the world was still, that head and bones came cascading into my consciousness. I managed to defeat their appearance most times, and being home helped immensely with this effort. The need to be with one's family during times of trouble cannot be underestimated. To me, the only good thing about this war was that it brought us together. I kept thinking about Bolek and his family and how they had invited us in and shared what little they had. That was a good thing. Poverty and degradation tend to take our own humanity from us. Generosity is a human trait, and to have this affirmed again was comforting.

Just before my mother cleared the dishes, she turned to me and said, "Mitchell, that boy—Wlacek—has been killed. He was trying to rob the Germans of their guns. They shot him."

"Oh no!" I gasped. While I was not a good friend of the boy, I did know him. He was not a lot different than me. We both were trying to take care of our families. The difference was that Wlacek's father had been killed, and he was the oldest of four children. He also was several years my senior, but when you are dead, this makes little difference.

"When?" I asked.

"Just after you left. The dirty Germans put his body in the doorway of the school," she said as her tears fell. My father reached to comfort her and said, "Come on, it will be all right. It was not Mitchell. He is not going to steal guns from the Germans anymore, are you, Mitch?"

Although it was phrased as a question, no answer was necessary. With the silence passing into discomfort, I said solemnly, "No, I won't do that anymore. But he was a good person. It's this war that makes us do these things..."

"I know."

The warning they were hoping to post resonated among the population, but I cannot say it endeared the Germans to us. Instead, our hatred continued to grow. Asking people to hate you is a sentiment I have never understood. I guess the Germans just thought that they were better than we were and because of this, considered us to be less than human. Therefore, our opinion of them mattered little. I think they preferred hatred and fear to acceptance. It seemed a difficult position to defend, but what could we do?

I thought about Wlacek for a long time that night. I knew why he was doing these things. If there had been sufficient food or if the Germans were not so cruel, perhaps things might have turned out differently. Again, if only. This war had the habit of generating an array of longings in our people. To dream of a world where the most momentous decisions were what girl you liked or what mom would be serving for supper that night was almost beyond our ability to comprehend. To live a life that was normal simply remained an unrealized dream. These longings were their own torment. Yet, they kept us alive inside.

With all that I have seen, I understand that death has a way of bringing our lives into focus. Death of someone near our own age does this even more potently. Wlacek deserved a chance to grow into a man. He was doing nothing that I had not done. In my mind, he was not doing anything wrong. Surviving is not wrong. Giving up and dying was. Given the choice between stealing and not stealing, when the result is either life or death, is not really a question that one debates for a long time.

For the next few months, our lives took on the patina of normality. Or at least what was passing for normal in those days. Nearly every night, around 2:00 AM, my father would wake me from bed, and we would go out in search of something that could help us survive for another day. Food was increasingly difficult to find. I was entering what should have been a growth spurt, but there was not enough food to nurture growth, let alone to maintain health.

I think the fact that my body was trying to grow so much made the deprivation worse for me than for adults. Children need to eat. Our bodies dictate this and we try, any way we can, to answer that call.

So, every night, when I should have been sleeping, I was walking in the stillness of the early morning, hoping to find some food from a passing German wagon or from farmers who had more than we did. This seemed to be a problem. The truth was no one was doing very well. Even those who had food did not have so much that they could afford this pilfering.

It was a bitterly cold winter. For days on end the snow would fall, and the thermometer would be stuck below freezing. It seemed as if summer, with its bounty, would never arrive.

Contrarily, we knew that the very best time to go out stealing was when the snow was falling or if there was a storm. The falling snow would sweep our footsteps under the cover of the snow. Consequently, on those days when the wind was howling and the snow falling sideways, we were out foraging and stealing whatever we could to survive.

In spite of my parents' best efforts, I continued to lose weight at the very time when I should have been gaining. I know that they always gave Andrew and me the best food and the greatest quantity. I understood that they would do without, if it would help us to grow. But more of too little is simply not enough. The sacrifices my parents were making were not unappreciated, but the fact remains that I was starving to death; we all were.

Both of my grandfathers were six feet four inches tall or better. My father was a large man, and I felt as if I were destined to be like them. But the lack of food was stifling my growth, and I knew it.

On those nights when we were not out stealing, I would lie in bed and listen to the wind, feeling the pain brought about by hunger. This pain is an incessant need that could not be met. It gives one a perspective on the world that is disquieting. I learned to loathe those who had enough to eat. This hatred translated into a total indifference as to whether they had any food left after we stole from them.

That winter, the winter of 1943, was the worst for me as far as hunger. Dinner would often consist of nothing more than a thin broth with a piece of "stuff" my mother called bread. It was dreadful. As I lay in bed at night, listening to the cold, I would think of those poor Russian prisoners we had seen. I was hungry, but not to that point yet. But I was close enough to look over the precipice into the depths of human degradation.

Often, when we went on an expedition to steal, we came back with little or nothing. Even a year ago there was more food available. Now, all that had been easy to steal was gone. Instead, there was little left that was not guarded or tightly secured. Occasionally we found a chicken, or an egg or two. But this is hardly enough food for a family in need.

We even tried stealing a piglet once. We knew, from earlier experience, that this was a bad idea. The little pigs make so much noise that they alert everyone to your presence. The night was perfect. Snow was falling, and there was a strong wind coming from the east. We crept to the edge of the paddock and climbed the fence quietly. My father opened the door to the barn, and I moved inside as quietly as I could. Even moving into the structure was odd. The wind, so prevalent outside, dissipated nearly immediately. I could hear the animals moving about, nervous at the intruder. I saw the sow with the piglets and reached over the stall and grabbed two of them, one in each hand and ran like hell.

The noise they put out was impressive. My father opened our bag, and I dumped them in as quickly as I could. But they kept up the squealing. Before we reached the road, the lights were on in the structure, and the farmer was running out screaming. We saw the lights come on in the police station, and we began running into the woods. All this time the piglets were making this horrendous noise. My father took the bag from my arms, but even he could not silence them. Finally, in desperation, he threw the bag aside. At about this time, the bullets started seeking us in the darkness.

Running as fast as we could worked, that time. The Gendarmes began following, but they soon lost their taste for the hunt as the snow got deeper and the wind keener. In a matter of moments, we heard them quit shooting, and the lights they carried pointed away from us.

I rested by my father and said, "Whew! That was close."

"It was. We had better move on. We are going to have to take the long way around. Are you too tired?"

"No, I can make it, Dad."

That night, we managed no food, but we did escape with our lives, and that was something. It would have been easy to give up, but we never did. We kept fighting against the specter of death that taunted us constantly.

Occasionally, the skies would clear, and the Russian

planes would return. The bombers would fly high in the sky surrounded by their fighter escorts. Suddenly they would begin to descend, and the Germans would open fire with their anti-aircraft guns. The fighters would come in low and fast with their guns strafing the German's positions. Then the bombers would let loose their ordinance, and the world would shake from their thunder.

It was odd when you woke in the morning, and it was clear. You knew that the planes would come that day bringing death with their bombs, death to the hated Nazis.

I watched their attacks so many times I knew exactly what they would do. They would approach the target so the sun was behind them. My father told me that this was to make the anti-aircraft guns miss. The fighters would strafe, and the bombers would loose their bombs. They fell with a terrifying shriek until ending their journey with a tremendous explosion. The Germans would try their best to bring them down with their machine guns, but firing into the sun is not easy. From our perspective, we were lucky. They spent most of their munitions attacking the trains at Jastrzabka rather than our small town. If they could not find a train, they would search for any German vehicle.

We were thankful that the bombers were not interested in the civilian population. The ever-present white handkerchief became an essential part of our attire, as much as a coat or shoes. When we spotted the planes, we took our white flags out and waved them wildly. With all of the ways to die in the war, we did not want to be victims of our friends.

Chapter 24

Throughout the degradation of that winter, our prayers were for an early spring. Finally, our petition to God was granted. In the middle of March the bitter winds ceased, and snow and ice began melting. The River Plodownica flooded the pastures with melted snow. It seemed a blessing to go outside without being bundled up so severely.

It took more than a month for the waters to recede and the pasture to dry. As it dried, the green grass returned, and the springtime flowers returned, punctuating the barrenness with exclamation marks of long-lost beauty.

In April, it rained nearly every day, renewing our world once more. The old grass had been beaten down by the rains and flood, but with each passing day, more new growth appeared until the field was dry enough for the animals to graze. Early in May, I began taking the cow to graze every day. It was beautiful and peaceful in the wide-open, grassy pasture with the crystal waters of the river murmuring softly in the background. It served as a poignant counterpoint to the deprivation and evil of the ever-present war.

The cow had lost so much weight during the course of the barren winter that she was dreadfully thin and no longer giving much milk. Truth was, she looked as much a walking skeleton as the rest of us. The first few times I took the cow out to the pasture, she was so weak she could hardly walk. I urged her on, and when we finally made it, I directed her away from last year's grass to the new growth. I pulled some green grass with my hand and fed her. On the way home from the pasture, I brought some of the grass with me and I continued to feed her. Walking alongside her with my hand gently touching her neck, I talked softly to her while urging her to eat more. She turned her head to me a few times, as though she were saying thanks.

Eating the new grass revived her considerably. It was hardly two weeks before she began getting frisky. It felt so good to watch her run a little and eat with such obvious pleasure. As her health improved and her milk production returned, it gave me a feeling of accomplishing something important.

The path to our house was well known to the cow, and I did not actually have to lead her. She knew the way, so I would walk alongside her. Occasionally, on our return journey home, I would see the German commissioner walking toward his house. He lived across the street from ours, and we would walk in the same direction. He could not speak a word of Polish, but he would look at me and probably wondered how I could get so attached to this animal.

The commissioner was a large, fat man who smiled easily. He seemed to be of a good nature and never bothered anyone. We always thought that he would not be a bad sort, if he did not have the SS watching him. The SS were always there, watching for any signs of weakness in the Germans.

On those early spring days, the German soldiers brought their horses to the pasture to graze. In broken Polish, they would command that we watch their animals for them. With the constant threat of Russian bombs, they could not afford to be seen in the open. We had to watch them so they wouldn't stray into farmers' fields.

Sometimes, as the sun would warm me and I would look into the blue skies, I would remember that terrible day of the previous year. Glancing toward the swamps on the other side of the river, I remembered that day when the mayor of our town decreed that the population had to forfeit all livestock to the German army for slaughter. My father told me to take the cow into the swamp and stay there until he told me that it was okay to come home.

I took our cow there and hid her for a long time. The swamp was a good place to hide because fog covered the area most of the time. I remembered how difficult it was to get the cow to walk through the muck. We moved from tussock to tussock and waited. Finally, word came from my father, and he helped me bring her home.

Often, while I was at the pasture watching the livestock, I would read. The Nazis had burned nearly all of the books, decreeing that people had to bring them to the center of town for a giant bonfire under the penalty of death. In spite of the door-to-door searches, my father had managed to find a few for me. One of my favorites at this time was Daniel Defoe's *Robinson Crusoe*. When the German soldiers left the pasture after giving us their horses, I read this book to my friends. They sat in a circle around me as I read the adventure story to them. They loved to hear about the strange world so far away.

To remind us, while we rested in the warm spring sun that there was a war, the Russian planes would appear several times each day, bombing the German outposts as the fighter planes strafed the German army repeatedly. We heard that the Russian planes and small fighters had bombed Jastrzabka, destroying the train station, railway and many supply wagons.

By June, with the warm weather, the temperature in the river warmed sufficiently for swimming. I did not know how to swim, but some of the other children taught me. The boys and girls who swam there would jump off a little bridge into the cold waters of the river; it was a lot of fun. With the warm weather and sufficient food and the fact that my family was together, I started to feel much better about my life.

There was a place on the river where the waters would

back up into a pool. Ringed with beautiful yellow water lilies and broad green leaves, the pool was a stagnant area teeming with fish. We made a makeshift net of two long sticks and some netting and tried our best to catch them. One day I managed to net a dozen good-sized fish. I took them home, and my mother cooked them. They were delicious.

Most days, because he was getting older, Andrew would come along. When he came, I had to watch him, the cow, the goats, and the German horses on occasion. It was a lot of responsibility. But he was becoming more and more company. We played together now—wrestling, laughing, and just having fun together. Because of this, we became very close. I liked having someone to talk with. He would stick close to me nearly always, and this gave me a good feeling. It got to the point where he wanted to go with me every place I went, and if I didn't take him with me, he got upset and threw a tantrum.

Later in the summer we would go into the fields, pick a few potatoes or carrots, build a fire, and bake them. That made life a little easier and more bearable. I liked to have my little brother with me, as he was good company.

That summer Mom and Dad went to work for farmers, digging potatoes and tying bundles of wheat. This kept us in bread, potatoes, and string beans for the summer, and we also prepared some food for the winter. Most of the food that was grown was taken away from the farmers and given to the Nazis. Whatever was left would have to last the winter. Food was a precious commodity.

When coming home from the pasture, we had to pass by one of the mass graves. As pleasant as the world seemed, it reminded me of how many relatives and friends I had lost in this war. When I thought of it, I could count twenty-one relatives and ten friends. Most of them had been tortured by the

Germans and then killed. A terrible loss for our family.

The summer of 1943 was a relatively enjoyable time in my young life. We did not see very many SS men. We did see German soldiers, but they had more important things to do than worry about than the poor people of Baranowo.

The soldiers would come and go. Most of them would stay in Baranowo for two or three months. Most of the German police assigned to our town were also new, except for a couple of them. The hated man who shot me in the head, Orzel, was still in the city hall, and I heard a lot of people say that his time is coming.

With the advent of autumn, we had to continue preparing for the winter. I helped my father dig holes to store the potatoes so we would have something to plant in the spring. I would start the hole where he indicated, but I would soon tire, and my father would take over.

In October, a group of local ladies came to my house to make sauerkraut. They sat in a large circle and shredded cabbage into a pile—all talking at the same time. For the life of me, I could not understand how they could keep track of so many conversations. I certainly could not.

When I listened, I just heard bits and pieces of conversation. There was one particular name that popped out of the cacophony, Placek. I heard that he had recovered from his injuries and was coming back to resume his duties. This scared me. He would know that I had escaped from the work camp. He also would know my father had escaped as well. The Germans thought I had escaped when I was digging peat moss. That conversation brought back bad memories about Placek. His piggish face flashed before my eyes and that hateful sneer lingered in my consciousness; I felt fear pierce through me like a jagged knife. I knew that if he came back, he would come after me. I could not get that thought out of my mind for the rest of the evening and most of the night.

Chapter 25

After a troubled sleep filled with the image of that dreadful, sadistic Placek, my father woke me and said, "Mitch, take the goats to that leafy glen by the pasture. Let them have their fill of the bark and shrubs there."

I yawned sleepily and got up. In the cool fall morning, with my father there, the vision of Placek vanished. After a small breakfast, I ventured out of the house to the barn and collected the goats. I always enjoyed working with my father. It gave me a feeling of accomplishment to finish the tasks he assigned to me.

I was glad to have him home with the family, and I felt more secure when he was with us. When he was around, he took care of these problems that seemed to constantly present themselves. Although I was learning self-sufficiency, having him there relieved me of those primary responsibilities. This was a good thing.

I took the goats through the frosty morning and spent the day with them at the edge of the communal pasture. During the day, I thought of the German police commandant often. No matter how I tried, I could not banish him from my mind. I knew that if he came back, my dad and I would have to go into hiding. Both of us had escaped from German labor camps, and Placek would be certain we were returned.

If we had to leave, then there would be no one to take care of Mom, my little sister Sophie, and Andrew. I was worried. Though the thought troubled me, there was little that I could do about it. I tried not to think about it. I was not successful.

The next day I helped my dad bury more potatoes and began the task of collecting both pine needles and pieces of wood for the winter fires. I carried large pieces of wood, as large as I could manage, and my father and I stacked them behind the barn.

My father busied himself with collecting peat moss and storing it for the winter. If nothing else, we would be warm. My father also brought in a large amount of hay and stacked it neatly in the barn. We worked hard at the preparations for the coming winter. Experience is a compelling teacher, and we had learned our lessons well. I did my jobs eagerly. It is very unpleasant to be either hungry or cold. Once you have been, it has been my experience that you will do what is necessary to avoid repeating the adventure.

Earlier I had stolen some jars from the pharmacy, and my mother soon filled these with green beans, carrots, and other vegetables. Hopefully, there would be enough to last us through the winter. The experience of the last year was still with us. This winter we would be better prepared.

On my way back from working in the fields, I noticed that the Germans had set up a large machine in the marketplace by our house. It looked almost like a locomotive, and it had an imposing chimney that belched black smoke into the crisp autumn sky. When I asked my father what the machine was, he replied, "A threshing machine of sorts. It separates the wheat from the chaff. They are going to collect the rest of the wheat that is still standing. Of course, I doubt they will share with us," he added sardonically.

The Germans seemed afraid to operate the machinery. The truth is that the Russian bombers and fighters were a major source of terror to the Germans. Every clear day, the planes would come and attack their positions. If they tried to move, their trucks were shot at and bombed. We had no direct news of how the war in Russia was going, but we could only assume that it was not going very well. If it had been going better, we doubted the Russians could claim the air superiority they obviously had.

After the Germans set up the machinery, they recruited—by force—Poles to run it. In addition to those who were actually working it, they collected whoever was in town at the time to stand around the machine so the Russians would not attack it.

Several days after the machine was operating, the weather cleared, and the day dawned gloriously. High in the sky we heard the sound of the approaching Russian planes. They came toward town, and the fighters drifted down and roared overhead, looking at the machine. They repeated this several times before the bombers attacked.

The Germans had set up anti-aircraft batteries nearby, and the still air was split with the ear-shattering noise of the machine guns firing, the planes diving, and the bombs exploding. So many bombs fell that it seemed as if the world were ending.

The machine was destroyed. The bombers also managed to hit the flour mill, and mostly destroy that. The noise was incredible. Every house in Baranowo had their windows broken out by the shockwave from the bombs. This was long before the era of precision bombing; the bombs fell everywhere in the city. It seemed the entire city was on fire.

People were running everywhere searching for cover. Blood streamed from their ears from the concussion of the bombs, and many of them were grievously injured. The Germans had made the local people prepare bomb shelters, but these were for the Germans. Everyone else had to hide wherever they could. And, in truth, there were few places to hide. We were at the mercy of the bombs.

The Germans continued firing the anti-aircraft guns, and the sky was full of puffs of smoke from the flak exploding in the air. The windmill that was on top of the hill about halfway to the forest was burning wildly.

Suddenly, the Russian fighters were confronted by the Luftwaffe. The German fighters shot down a Russian bomber. I saw a Russian fighter plane ram a German fighter plane; it looked as though he had intentionally steered that final course. I asked my dad about this, and he explained, "They will do that when they are out of ammunition. Brave men."

Within fifteen minutes, one third of Baranowo was destroyed and burning. The Russians seemed satisfied with their bombing and headed back to the East. In the silence that followed, we heard the screams of the injured. Many, many people were killed in that attack. More were hurt.

There was no doctor to help the wounded, just German army doctors who helped their own. Feltzer, the veterinarian, tried to take care of as many people as he could, but without medical supplies he couldn't do much. The people who were critically injured died. My neighbor lost her sixteen-year-old daughter and her little boy. Almost every family in town lost someone. My Aunt Mary and her eight-year-old child were killed in the attack. It was a terrible time of great sadness in Baranowo.

Our family survived this air raid more-or-less intact. We did lose one goat, but with all of the death and destruction that befell others, we felt fortunate. A corner of our house was blasted open, but my father repaired it. The planes had destroyed the German machine, most of the windmill, and the flourmill. The flourmill and windmill were repaired, but we never saw the giant thresher again.

When Christmas came, my mom and dad took our family to Midnight Mass. We stayed in the church until daylight with many of our friends and neighbors, singing carols and praying. The importance of the church in these bad times cannot be underestimated. The church was full night and day during the Christmas season. It truly did seem a place of sanctuary from an oppressive world.

We came home early in the morning, and Mom fixed us kasza for breakfast. The cereal was warm and tasted good. Christmas was peaceful even though we didn't have a Christmas tree or enough to eat. I knew that I could get used to this peaceful and joyous time. My mom sang Christmas songs as we all sat in the living room. Even Andrew and Sophie listened intently. It was such a special time that I will never forget. It is still with me now.

My mother had set up a picture of the Madonna holding the Christ child and had a candle burning there during the entire Advent season. As she sang, I prayed to God to deliver my family from this dreadful war. And even though Christmas could have been more special, we realized that having us together and safe was something worth appreciating.

The time following Christmas was peaceful. If we were still hungry, we were less so than a year ago. Our family was together, and the shock of the air raid that killed so many had worn off. Our grieving ebbed into an acceptance that the living needed to be tended now. For a while I almost forgot this dreadful war. There were occasional flashes of the sadness and hatred I had witnessed, but I was managing to put these down. Every day I thanked the Lord for still being alive and being with my family.

I was growing very fond of my new sister and my brother. They seemed to feel the same way about me. Andrew followed me everywhere I went, and I liked it. It made me seem important to have the responsibility of watching over Andrew and occasionally Sophie. I felt as though I were on my way to becoming an adult. This was pleasant, a peaceful transition from childhood to being an adult. Not like the forced adulthood I had experienced earlier when my father was taken from me, and I was placed in the position of being responsible for my family. This was different, and better.

Three days after the New Year had been celebrated, two German soldiers came to live in our house. They were noncommissioned officers, and they took one of our bedrooms over. Later they brought a sophisticated radio and set it up in their room. Sometimes they talked into it, but it was nearly always on whether they were there or not. For months we listened to the radio. My father understood some German and was able to glean a great deal of information in this way.

He told me that the American forces were advancing into Germany and that there had been some sort of tremendous uprising in Warsaw. We were not given any details, but the news of the American army was glad tidings. My father believed that the Americans would end the war and restore peace in Poland and other countries.

Having the German soldiers in our house was not without benefit. The two men learned to appreciate my mother's potato pancakes and often brought potatoes for her to use. They also brought us flour, and this helped us survive. The winter was passing, and we knew spring was coming.

In June my biggest nightmare came true. Placek returned.

My dad went into hiding. He hugged us tightly and simply left. He did not tell us where he was going, and we did not ask. It was not in anyone's interest to know this information. Our tears fell that day, but there was no choice. We would have to get along as best we could. The only good thing was that with the summer, we stood a better chance of surviving without his assistance.

I was going to get out too, but where could I go? My mother and I talked about it, and we decided to chance staying at home. Perhaps the Germans would forget about me. After all, I was a mere boy of 11.

We thought this. We might have even believed it. But

within several days of Placek's return, the SS came to our house early in the morning and knocked forcefully. I looked out of the window and saw who it was. I wanted to run, but there were the two soldiers in the house who prevented this.

The Gendarmes had been told that I was here, and they were looking for me. When they saw me, I was hit and kicked repeatedly. My mother pleaded with them to leave me alone. One of the SS men hit her viciously in the face with the butt of his rifle. She fell and did not get up.

As they dragged me kicking and screaming out of the door, I kept looking at my mother lying on the floor unconscious and praying that she would be okay. I tried to run back to help my mom. One of the SS men kicked me in the throat. I fell in agony. I was conscious but could hardly breathe. I was panic-stricken. I thought I was going to die. I did not know if my mother was okay. It was dreadful.

While I was holding my throat, they dragged me to the truck and threw me in the back with other men and boys they had collected that morning. I was taken to a labor camp.

Chapter 26

When I was in the back of that truck, I did not talk. I simply sat and massaged my throat. I was having difficulty breathing; rubbing it seemed to help. My thoughts at this time were dark. I did not know what was going to happen, but my fear was real. I had been in a labor camp; they were without virtue. I had no idea of how terrible this one would be, or I might have leapt from the truck and died.

I was taken to a small labor çamp and directed to a barracks for confinement. The German guard looked at me and then read a note that someone had written on a piece of paper. In broken Polish he said, "Because you have escaped before, you will not be allowed the privilege of shoes or even a shirt. If you try to escape this time, you will be killed. In the most unpleasant way we can think of." He looked at me for an answer, but what could I say? I said nothing.

Every day they woke us, and we were taken to the fields where we dug trenches and foxholes for the Nazis. It was clear from this activity that they had no intention of leaving our area peacefully.

It seemed a shame to tear up farmers' fields while they were trying to grow wheat and potatoes, but we had no choice. Working in the fields digging, without shoes, was hard on my feet. Day after day they got worse until they were bleeding nearly all of the time. They hurt terribly, but I had no choice. I continued working no matter how much pain I was in. The Nazis did not suffer that anyone not work. The alternative was a sure and swift death. Each day became a new experience in agony.

Because the ground was hard, we used picks and shovels to dig the holes. It was extremely difficult work for a young boy. I was so tired by the end of the day that I could not imagine doing the same thing the next day. As I lay on my pallet, a simple board without covers or mattress, I prayed for my deliverance and the safety of my family. At least at first, toward the end of my confinement, I simply wished for death.

We were continually exhausted from working. The Nazis continued to be cruel taskmasters. They would beat us for no reason in particular. I think they simply liked doing it. For example, if one of the boys stretched his body to relieve his aching muscles, the whip would strike him mercilessly. And this whip was a huge braided leather whip used for horses. The sound of that whip shrieking through the air, with the snap when it hit is with me always. I remember watching the whip strike the boys and seeing the welt form immediately. Because we all had been whipped so often, more times than not the whip opened old sores, and the blood would spatter with the contact. It was a brutal oppression.

Though most of the guards were German nationals, there were a few Ukrainian men who had endeared themselves to the Germans. Over my group was a particularly nasty man named Ivan. Ivan was a terrible, sadistic person. He would whip us severely for no reason whatsoever. And the smile on his face as he did it was simply ghastly. I know now that men like this are called sadists. They derive satisfaction from being cruel. At that time I did not understand such things and only knew that he was a nasty man who enjoyed his position of power and had a particular dislike for me.

When he was not whipping us, he would tease us endlessly. While we were working, he would pick up clods of dirt or stones and hit us with them. Not a gentle, playful hit; but he threw them with such authority that they hurt terribly. When we turned to see who had done such a thing, he would laugh loudly and smile at us. His smile was insidious.

Most of the beatings I received, and there were many, were done for his amusement and not for punishment. We understood what was expected of us, and we did our best to comply. To Ivan, it made little difference. He would simply begin whipping us without mercy, flaunt that dreaded smile, and laugh at us writhing in pain.

I felt thoroughly insulted and degraded, but the intense pain masked the mental agony. If I made him a little angry and avoided him, he would run to me and place a few kicks in my stomach, while screaming vulgar obscenities and calling me a worthless swine. Since I didn't have any clothes on except for some torn shorts, he would grab me by the testicles and squeeze as hard as he could all the while giggling and laughing. My screams from these violations echoed in the stillness, but died on the winds of indifference. I learned to hate him and wished for some sort of revenge.

The pain I felt was constant. My body ached from the work. My feet were constantly swollen and bleeding. My skin was unprotected from the elements, and the rain and heat and sun had done much damage.

Because I was in such pain, my sense of humor, which I had used many times for self-defense, failed me. Try as I might, I could find no humor in this situation. I was nearly naked, worked like an animal, and punished mercilessly. I felt I was reaching the end of my tether. I had never before experienced such desolation of the soul. Honestly, I began to believe that it would be better to just lie down and die. I simply cannot tell you how horrific this experience was. Words fail me.

With every movement, every time I walked, the pain assaulted me. I felt completely helpless, and pleasant thoughts of suicide entered my mind. The silent screams returned. Oddly enough, these helped some. I did not make a noise, but in my mind I cried to my Lord for deliverance. I screamed the desolate silent scream of agony.

Some of the prisoners dreamed about food, loved ones, and their parents. I did too, but I also dreamed of exacting revenge on the sadistic Ivan. The thought went through my mind often asking how much I can endure if this keeps up. I believed that I would either go insane or die; there simply were not many choices.

But as the silent screams of agony helped, so did the fantasy of revenge on Ivan. I imagined doing all sorts of cruel things to this man. A cruelty for every time he was cruel to me. The thought began to consume me. Even while I was working and the whip was whistling, I would imagine what it would feel like to hurt him.

I also dreamed of escaping. But with no shoes or clothes and the guards watching us closely, this seemed impossible. The Russian planes and the fighters would fly overhead, and we chanced a glance at them while we worked. I think I might have even prayed that they attack us. At least if they did that, in the confusion I might be able to get away—if I survived the bombs. But I was in such misery that this seemed to be of little importance as well.

By now, my mind had deteriorated to the point where nearly every thought was either of dying or revenge. I still lived on, after a fashion, and I am grateful to God for this. I feel like I am still living, but somehow dead. I pray for the miracle that will rescue me from this cruel purgatory of the soul, for all I know is extreme misery and severe depression.

One day as guards marched us to dig a bunker, we were mixed with the older prisoners to help cut down trees to line the bunkers we had dug. The older prisoners were given the task of actually felling the trees while the boys were set to the task of removing the branches. After the men had prepared enough logs for the bunker, we started digging it.

We heard that the Russians were beating the Germans and they were getting closer. We also heard bits and pieces about the Warsaw uprising. Russian planes were bombing Germany almost every day, and we did not see many German planes flying. Someone said they were running out of gasoline. These rumors and thoughts of misery befalling our enemies encouraged us slightly. It did not help our situation immediately, but it did give us hope for the future, something that had been missing for a long time.

As the sun began to set and our quitting time was near, I was so tired that I stretched my body to relieve the agony. Almost immediately, I felt the whip strike me mercilessly. The pain I felt inflamed me, and I turned to see who had struck me. It was Ivan, sneering and laughing maliciously.

He moved closer to me and kicked me as hard as he could in the stomach. I fell to the ground. My hand chanced upon a sharpened stick. I smiled grimly as I felt my fingers close around the broken wood.

When Ivan bent over to grab my testicles, I mustered enough strength to get up half way with the stick in my right hand. Looking at him with total hatred in my mind, I took the stick and thrust it deep into his eye. I pushed it in as far as I could. I felt it ease through the eye and then encounter something hard. I let it go as he began howling and screaming. I watched him as he danced about screaming and trying to pull the stick out of his eye. I smiled as I saw the blood running down his face.

My instinct for survival told me to run. There were only two German guards with guns, and they were on the other end of the field. I bolted away as fast as I could downhill. My heart was beating rapidly, and I felt an adrenalin rush as I ran. The adrenalin helped to ease the pain, as I ran faster and faster.

When I heard the gunshots, I ran even faster. I was scared,

but I knew that the guards couldn't leave the other inmates because they would run away. I didn't stop running until I came to a small farmhouse. I saw some clothes hanging out to dry and helped myself to a pair of pants and a shirt. I kept running through the alleys of the town until I reached the other side where there was a small patch of trees just before the river. I stopped and looked behind me to see if I was being followed. When I was sure I wasn't, I put the pants on. They were too long and too large around the waist. But there was a tear-hole in the knee of the pants, so I tore the fabric strarting at the hole and around the pant leg. I made the pants shorter and put them on. I found a piece of vine to use for a belt and put on the shirt and stuffed the excess into the pants.

  The vision of Ivan, with the stick protruding from his eye, formed in my mind as I walked. I have wrestled with this incident in my mind many times. I finally have justified the incident by calling it self-defense. If I had stayed, I am certain that I would have died like many others. I chose to survive. A decision I have never regretted.

Chapter 27

I left the town and walked along the country road for a couple of kilometers. I was not sure of where I was, but I knew that I was not safe in a town. The German police would probably have been alerted to my escape and would be scouring the towns looking for me. I did not know if my attack had killed Ivan, but I was certain that I had wounded him severely. I knew that if I were caught, I would be punished.

As I came over a hill, I saw a small Polish farm. The house was made of logs, and the roof was thatched. There was a barn and a paddock. I started going toward it with the idea of knocking on the door and asking for help. This was not unusual in that time. Many times, at our house, we had helped strangers. It was an aspect of communal intimacy accentuated by being an occupied country.

As I stared at the house, trying to decide whether to approach it, I noticed that there was a horse with a saddle in front. This did not seem right. Polish people rode their horses bareback. Besides, it was night, and the horse should have been in the barn by that time.

My father's words came back to me, "If something does not seem right, go back, examine everything, and see what is wrong." I cautiously approached the house and moved my way around it in the dark. At the back, I found two more horses with saddles. The knowledge came to me then, "These must be the Gendarmes' horses!" I backed away carefully, crossed into the woods, and continued on my way.

This was very difficult for me to do as I was not in good shape. The whippings had taken their toll; my feet were cut and bleeding; and I still had no shoes. I traveled for another three kilometers or so through the pastures and forest.

I was so tired that I stopped to rest for a moment. As I sat at the edge of the forest in the pasture, I closed my eyes. Even with my eyes closed tightly, I could see the face of Ivan, the Ukrainian guard, as he danced about screaming in agony—the stick protruding from his eye. I thought to myself, 'Why did I lose control?' I thought that maybe I could have survived another beating; I had done so before. For a moment I imagined how it would feel to have a stick in my eye. I dismissed the thought because it was too terrible to even to think about. I continued walking and thinking. I decided, that after all, the bastard deserved it. What he did to me was not necessary under any rules governing human conduct.

Living through this tortuous war had taught me to ignore the minor discomforts of hunger and cold. I forced myself to get up and started walking again. I came upon a small road, and I knew there must be a farm nearby.

I kept walking and crossed a bridge over an irrigation ditch. I heard cows and chickens behind the bushes and trees, and I knew I was right. I walked a little farther and saw a house with a barn and some outbuildings. The house stood just outside a stand of tall pine trees.

I approached the house carefully. There was something about the place that was familiar, but I could not determine what it was. It was like I recognized it. But how could that be?

When I knocked on the door, a middle-aged woman came to the door and asked, "Yes, what can I do for you?" She looked at me and saw immediately my poor condition. She stepped out of the door and looked around suspiciously. "Are you alone?"

"Yes, I am. I escaped from a work camp."

"Come in, come in and warm yourself. What is your

name? Wait! You are Mitch Garwolinski from Baranowo, right?"

I recognized her. This was Kasia and Jan's house, the same people who had saved my life when I escaped from the work camp, the same good people who nursed me back to health when I had been so sick. She hugged me tightly and ushered me inside.

She pointed toward a wooden cot where a one-armed man was laying on a straw mattress and said, "Jan, do you remember Mitch Garwolinski from Baranowo?" Jan greeted me warmly, "Mitch, Mitch—so good to see you. Come in and be welcome."

Kasia led me toward the table and whispered, "Jan was a partisan with the Underground before his injuries." I looked and the man was grievously wounded. One arm was gone, and the side of his body and face were horribly scarred.

I even remembered their last name, Zima. I felt much more at home almost immediately. There was a fire in their homemade stove. The woman gave me some milk and a piece of freshly baked bread. Bustling around the kitchen, she also served me a bowl of chicken soup. I was so hungry that the food tasted simply wonderful.

I thought I was in heaven. When I was eating the food, I noticed a teen-age boy and girl come out of another room. They watched me eat. The woman said, "Take it easy. You will get sick to your stomach. Take it nice and slow."

I tried. I honestly did. But being warm, the companionship of friends, and hot food was almost more joy than I could take.

When I was finished, she asked me lots of questions about my family and how I ended up at their home again. I answered her questions as best I could. When I was finished, she hugged me and said, "This war, it makes us do things we normally would never do. Don't worry too much about Ivan.

It seems he got what he deserved."

I wanted to move on that night. I felt that my being in their house presented a danger. I knew the Germans would be looking for me. But Kasia and Jan would not even consider my leaving. They prepared a bed for me and told me to sleep till morning. There would be time to discuss what to do then.

We all said a prayer, and I soon fell into a deep sleep. During the sleep I dreamed about Ivan and the labor camp from which I'd I escaped. I must have yelled or talked in my sleep because Kasia woke me and consoled me telling me. "It is only a dream, Mitch. Go back to sleep." I finally did.

Actually, during this time, I remember waking, screaming many times. It was during sleep that the full impact of the situation was understood, but it was good to hear this woman's pleasant voice. And and when she left me to go back to sleep, it didn't take very long. With the help of friends, there might be a possibility that I could find a way to get away from this area. Maybe I could even make it to Grabownica and stay with my aunt and uncle and the Jewish families my dad and I took there in the beginning of the war. I thought that maybe my father had gone there. But it was not meant to be.

In the morning, I was awakened by a sharp kick in my side and a harsh voice saying, "Wake up, you little pig."

I looked up and saw that the house was full of German police. Some of them had black uniforms with a skull and crossbones on their hats—the hated SS. One policeman had me by the neck. Another put my hands behind my back, cuffed me, and then chained them to my feet. They carried me out of Jan and Kasia's house and threw me in the back of a truck covered with green canvas. They were laughing and saying, "You will never escape again, you little pig." I recognized the one who said this as Placek's man. As I was lying on the bed of the truck, one of the Nazis SS officers shot Jan in the head. The man roughly bound the children and Kasia and threw them into the back of another truck.

Lonely, hopeless, and terrifying feelings came over me as I watched the Zimas' home disappear through the back of the truck. I did not know where I was going, and I was scared.
I had terrible feelings about this. I thought about poor Mr. Zima, lying dead, and I wondered why the Nazis didn't take him with his family. "Why did they shoot him?" Then I knew. The fact that he was crippled had made him useless to them. I tried to imagine how his family must be feeling. Waves of sorrow rushed over me.
This was such a kind family; I felt overwhelmed and was so sorry for them. It must have been horrific to see their father killed. I wondered what was going to happen to me and where were they taking me. Thoughts of my own family passed through my mind, but I knew that I was on my own now. Ivan, the Ukrainian guard, flashed through my mind, along with many other things I had done. I thought, "My God! I am becoming an animal." I certainly seem to have acquired animal instincts and had a sensation in my heart that I would not come out of this alive.
There was a Nazi SS guard sitting near me in the back of the truck. He was leaning back and looking at me occasionally. I did not like his smile. The ride was very bumpy, especially with chains on. I noticed that the other vehicles went in the opposite direction from mine, and I wondered why. Where were they taking me? I was feeling weak, hungry, and still in pain from the kick this man guarding me delivered to my ribs to wake me. I asked the SS man with the deep eyes and deadly smirk, "Where are they taking me?"
He didn't answer. I tried again, "Where are they taking me?"
"Shut up, you Polnische banditen!"
I did not repeat the question.

Chapter 28

That morning is etched forever in my mind. I remember each shudder of the truck as it encountered a rough spot in the road. Every pothole, every bridge. They are all a part of me now. The road was rough initially, but after about an hour, it smoothed considerably. I tried to watch out of the back of the truck to see if I could determine where I was. The towns had names, but they were unfamiliar to me.

I remembered when my father talked to the man in Jastrzabka. He had told my father that, in addition to the large well-known concentration camps, there were many, many more. These were located all over Poland and Germany. I remembered a few of them like Brandenburg, Norhousen, Dora, Ravensbrook, Treblinka, and the biggest hell of all (Poswiecim), Auschwitz. I had not seen any sign that resembled these.

We must have passed a labor camp, because I heard a familiar Nazi whistle pierce the monotony of the road. I looked out of the back and saw the Germans screaming and hitting the boys and young men in their custody.

The further that we drove, the more nervous I was getting. Every minute seemed an eternity. I was miserable, the need to relieve my bladder was increasing, and this was made worse by each bump in the road. The driver had already stopped the truck twice to relieve himself, but they did not afford me the same opportunity. I was simply a Polish pig to them.

Finally, the driver stopped again, and my guard stepped out of the truck to relieve himself. After he was finished, he unchained one of my wrists and helped me out of the back of the truck. When I was done, my hand was chained again, and I was tossed back into the truck.

We started down the road again. After a short amount of time, I saw my guard step to the back of the truck and scream, "Schwein Jude" at the prisoners working in the fields. I knew that this meant "Jewish pig" so we must be close to a concentration camp. I still had no idea of where I was.

I found myself going deeper into my own mind again. I remembered when my father had been taken away to labor camp. He had been gone a long time, and finally someone told my mother that he had been killed by the Gestapo. My mom had not told me, and I didn't know why she was often crying. I finally asked, "Mom, where is Dad?" She looked at me and grabbed me by my shoulders. With tears in her eyes and trying to force a small smile, she answered, "My son, your dad was killed in a labor camp."

When mom told me that, I screamed, and the tears came running down my cheeks. I sobbed while my mother mingled her tears with mine and held me.

The idea that my father was dead was an oppressive weight being placed upon me. It just couldn't be! I screamed in my mind, "My father is not dead!"

Dad was my best friend. I loved him; I felt a sense of security when he was around. I did not know how we could get on without him. I felt so weak and helpless for a long time.

I knew that we had to survive somehow. I tried to think of what I could do to help. All of this time, the reality of my father's passing was working its way into my consciousness. I think that is when I truly began to mature.

In order to make Mom feel better, I said, "Mom, I'll go far away where they have big farms, and I'll make a deal to work there. I'll support us."

"Okay, my dear son. Here, take this little cross." I

watched as she removed the chain from her neck and placed the chain and gold cross around mine. She looked me in the eye as she was attaching it and said, "If poverty, cold, and hunger hurt you, please come back to our poor and humble little house."

"I will. I promise."

Just before I was planning on leaving, my father came home. I was never so glad to see anyone in my life. I had given up hope that he would ever return. It was a glorious day. The feeling of that day has propelled my life since. I think, in a way, that accounts for my ability to survive. I believe in the future.

A train whistle brought me back to reality as the truck was pulling into the station and came to a stop. The guard jumped off the truck and told me, "Come over here!" I moved to comply, but maneuvering with the chains constricting my limbs was difficult. The guard came and roughly pulled me toward a building alongside the station.

When we walked in the room, there were two small desks several soldiers. The men were mostly SS officers, and their insignias burned into my mind. The guard handcuffed me to a steel bench and said something to a high-ranking Nazi in a black uniform. I think he was a captain, and I heard the word "Hoffman." His insignia was one that I did not recognize.

The man looked at me with those cold eyes that examine you as if you are no more than animal. I had seen that look before, and it frightened me. I knew that I was in for a lot of trouble and pain. When I considered the pain, I nearly panicked. I did not believe I could take anymore. The guard left.

I looked out the window and saw a train at the station. Guards were posted on both sides, watching the boxcars packed with people as if they were cattle. I remembered that terrible morning when the young Jewish woman threw the little baby off the train. That scene had replayed itself in my memory so many times that it had become a part of my being.

And in that instant, I understood the reason the woman had thrown the baby off the train and rushed into the bullet herself. Hunger! Hunger is the most nagging torture. It is insidious that so many both Jewish and Polish people would rather die than starve.

I have seen people charging their guards and falling in a hail of bullets so they would not have to suffer anymore. It is hard to understand. In fact, that feeling is beyond my meager abilities with the language to describe. It permeates your soul in ways that are so damning that everything in your life becomes insignificant by comparison. The need to eat. The need to survive is a strong one, and when we deny this, sometimes the person would simply rather die. The need to not feel pain can overcome the need to survive. I knew this.

Another transport passed on the other side of the train that was standing at the station. After the transport train passed, the one that was loading started moving. The steam engine began belching faster and faster, the driving wheels moved forward at a quickening pace, and the train was gone.

After the train left, I saw some Jewish and Polish prisoners working on the tracks. They were not close, so I could not see what they were doing, but the bright yellow Star of David and the large letter P could clearly be seen.

The German guard yelled at the men and occasionally struck them with the whip or kicked them with his heavy boot. As I watched the scene unfold, I knew what they were feeling, and it was terrible. I also knew that my concerns were useless. There was nothing I could do to help them. I knew, in my heart, that I had better start thinking of myself.

It was late in the afternoon already, and I was hungry. I had not had anything to eat since the previous night. I glanced out of the window and tried to see where I was again. As hungry as I was, I wanted to know my location. It was important to me.

A German soldier brought some food for the two men sitting behind the desks. They didn't even look at me while they ate their food with great relish. Through the stagnant air of the building, I could smell what they were eating, and my mouth started watering. I did not want to, but I had a difficult time in drawing my eyes from the food. I was so hungry!

After they finished their lunch, they smoked a cigarette and talked. I don't know what they said, but they both started laughing while they looked at me. I was too tired and hungry to even think. I slumped down beside the bench on the floor and lay there.

In truth, I had not yet recovered from the last labor camp. I was weak, and the months of near starvation had taken their toll. I had lost so much weight I looked sick. I closed my eyes and tried to forget. Sleep claimed me until a train whistle woke me.

I turned my head to the two Nazis; the guard was looking at me off and on as he finished eating something else. He threw the remainder of his sandwich on the floor between us. I dove for it. I was so hungry. But he had thrown it just out of reach. As I stretched for it, he got up from his seat and pushed the sandwich closer with the toe of his boot so that I could reach it. As I stretched out my hand, he stomped on my hand with his boot and brutally held it there.

While he was standing on my hand, I looked at his face. Those cold eyes were there again. I screamed in agonizing pain. The Nazi looked down at me and smiled sadistically. The other Nazi said something in German to the one standing on my hand. I could understand a couple of the words. He said, "If you break his hand, he will not be able to work."

"What? You feel sorry for this Polish pig?"

"No, but if you break his hand, he will not be able to work. That is all."

He finally stepped off of my hand, looked at me, and said, "Polnisches Schwein." I jumped to my feet just as another officer entered the room. I tried to look out of the window of the door before it closed again. I was not tall enough. The arriving officer got the key to my chain from the desk, came over, and unlocked my chain from the metal bench while holding it firmly. "Schnell gekommen!"

We walked to the front door; this time the guard walked fast, yanking me by the chain as if he didn't want me to look back. I turned and tried to see the station name. I could not.

He practically pulled me all the way to the transport train. He roughly removed the chains and threw me into a boxcar full of kids like me and smaller.

There was no roof on the car, but the walls were very high. After I heard the door slide to the boxcar, the train began moving. I looked at my companions on this journey. Most were my age or younger. Some were even thinner than I was—something I hardly believed possible.

I saw some boys about my age and asked, "Where are we going?" One of the boys looked at me and then at the ground. Finally, he said, "There are rumors. One is that we are on our way to Auschwitz-Birkenau in Poland." Another boy disagreed, "No, we are headed for the experimental hospital. I don't know the name, but I know it is not far from here."

I slumped against the wall of the car. This fearful news made me shudder. I had heard of the Nazi place for kids, the place where they would finally send them if they couldn't be converted into Nazis. At these places doctors would take their blood and perform experiments on their bodies. When they had used them completely, they would kill them by slicing the bottoms of their feet with a scalpel and let them bleed to death in their beds.

The night was cold and dark; rain started cutting into our faces as we traveled toward the unknown.

Chapter 29

After an hour of rough motion, the train began slowing. This portion of the journey had been accomplished in near silence from those of us sitting on the floor of the roofless boxcar, shivering in the cold rain. In truth, none of us could think of anything to say. Besides, we were caught up considering our own secret dreads. As the train slowed, I looked at my companions. I wanted to say something, anything, to ease the terrible feeling of impending doom we all felt, but there was nothing to say. From the silence, I knew that everyone felt this way.

When the train had stopped completely, I asked the tallest boy if I could stand on his shoulders and try and look over the side of the car. He agreed and moved to the side and interlocked his fingers to help me get up. I tried. I honestly did. But I was too weak to stand on his shoulders, and he was too weak to hold me. We both fell on the rain-soaked floor of the car.

The door creaked open loudly, and a basket with loaves of bread was shoved inside. The door closed immediately with a resounding clang that echoed in the stillness. We passed the bread around, making certain that those too weak to come and get their own got their portion first. We knew who they were; when they tried to stand, they staggered and fell. We gave them their loaves and then ate ourselves.

As I sat and ate my bread in the locked boxcar awaiting my fate, my mind considered some of what I had seen in my lifetime. I was weak and getting weaker, I knew this. But weakness to the Nazis was simply a reason to kill, so I tried not to show it. The Nazis were the most cruel people you can imagine. I could remember watching the SS men kicking and beating people through the streets of Baranowo. If one happened to pass out from the pain, they brought him to consciousness again, so they could repeat their cruelty.

They were especially brutal to the Jewish people when they wanted information. I had seen them, in public places, tie these poor people's hands behind their backs and then hang them on a hook. I could hear their screams as their shoulder muscles tore.

The Nazis, not even satisfied with this most fiendish torture, would then proceed to break their bones—legs, fingers, arms—as their screams would rip the air. I hated them. I say that without remorse. I know that as a Christian, I am not supposed to hate. But are they supposed to act like this?

I had witnessed these poor people confessing to anything and everything. They simply wanted the pain to stop. Sometimes they would beat them as long as two hours. But most often it was much less as the people being tortured would pass out, and the Nazis would not be able to bring them to consciousness again.

I continued eating the stale bread and remembering. When I was in the work camp the first time, there was a man named Ciuba. Ciuba was always happy. Nothing seemed to bother him, and even the disgusting treatment that we received failed to dampen his spirit. I liked him, and his smile seemed to make our situation a little bit better.

One day, no different than any other day, the Gestapo took him for interrogation. I believe it was just before noon when they took him. When they returned him the next evening, he was a changed man. When he had gone with them, he had done so with great confidence. He knew that he had done nothing wrong, and it was his assumption that if he had done nothing wrong, he would not be punished. He was wrong.

When he returned, he needed assistance from the other prisoners to make it to his cot. He was beaten so badly. We helped to dress his wounds. He had cuts and bruises over much of his body, but the Nazis had seemed to concentrate on his head. His body was black and blue from the beatings and covered with welts from the whipping he had received. Even more ominously, a broken bone stuck out from his lower leg, bloody and white.

After seeing these viciously inflicted wounds, I found it hard to believe any human could go through this and survive. But I also had difficulty comprehending how one human could inflict such punishment on another. Meanwhile, we put bandages on his wounds, gave him some aspirin that someone had, and a cigarette. We didn't have many medical supplies; this was all that we could do for him.

That night, we took turns watching over him and offering what comfort we could. When it was my turn, I got down on my knees and prayed for him to survive. He was a good man and certainly did not deserve such treatment.

In the morning, he felt a little better. At least well enough to talk about what he had experienced. He said, "They bound my hands behind my back; the guards beat me with a chair. When I could stand no longer, they began kicking me. All of the time they were demanding that I tell them about Polish people who were conspiring against the Germans and hiding Jews. I did not know anyone, but they did not believe me. When they got tired of kicking me, they took their whips and struck me so many times, I passed out."

He started crying a little, and we waited while he regained his composure. After a few moments he continued, "They took me to a cell without a floor, just cold mud. Hours later, after I had regained consciousness, they took me back to the interrogation room and repeated their tortures. With my body already torn up by the whipping, the second whipping was more terrible than the first, and I did not maintain my consciousness for very long. I passed out. Once more I was allowed to recover; when I had, they took me back to the interrogation room and started again. I finally told them three names of people who were conspiring against them. Honestly, I don't know anyone who is, so I made up the names. They seemed satisfied, and that is when they brought me back here."

He slept again, and when he would not regain consciousness, the Nazis brought him back to the barracks. All I know is that he was a broken man in body and spirit.

As I sat in the boxcar thinking of these things, the cold rain began falling harder. We heard shouts, and the train lurched ahead. It seemed as though we had stopped at this train station for about an hour.

We could not see what was going on, but we thought they were loading more people into the boxcars. I curled into a fetal position against the wall, as did most of the others, and continued to shiver from the cold rain that had been coming down for hours. Many of us were suffering from hypothermia, although we didn't know it at the time.

The train was finally moving, and I tried to calm my fears. Sometimes I would daydream in order to escape into sort of a paradise, but now I was too exhausted to even do that. I couldn't fall asleep. The daydreams and my sense of humor had always helped to protect me from this inhumane treatment, but they were no longer working. Before I could nearly always find a mental place of escape. I liked to hear the birds sing and see the flowers growing larger day by day. Most of all, I yearned to hear the voices of my mom and dad. At that point I would have given almost anything to hear the voice of anyone in my family.

It was hard to believe, but all of us on that car dozed off until the train whistle woke us up. The sun was shining now, but we still didn't know where we were or where we were going. The train came to a halt, and the doors opened. A group of SS men greeted us with a diatribe of expletives in German and the command to "Max schnell, schnell!"

We were half asleep when the doors opened, so the Germans had to help us out of the car. They did this with their rifle butts and the ever-present leather horsewhips. Most of us fell out of the cars instead of jumping and landed on the stone railroad bed. The Nazis kicked us as we lay there and began swinging their whips at us to get us to move more quickly.

In case any of the sick and hunger-weakened children were to pose a threat to them, they had their Alsatian dogs accompanying them—teeth bared and held back from ripping us to pieces by the guards.

I was hit several times with the whip and kicked repeatedly. One time the whip stung my back, and the end wrapped around my neck and landed on my throat with a tremendous burst of pain. I screamed. They did not care.

I was in severe pain and fear; plus my breathing was affected. Even though I was in the midst of many people, I had never felt quite so alone. I honestly felt that God simply did not care what happened to us. I called his name anyway, praying for deliverance.

After we all practically fell off the wagon, I noticed that the next few wagons were full of grown men. Their wagons had roofs and metal bars on the windows. I observed for a brief moment, and I noticed that the men's treatment was worse than ours. The SS were hitting them with the rifle butts and with whips. They were kicking the men on the ground who had jumped to avoid the punishment. They were holding theirs hands up, trying to protect their heads from the rifle butts and the whistling leather whips. None of these poor men made it safely to the ground without getting hit. Most of theirs heads were bleeding. They were in appalling condition.

No more than skin and bones, they looked like living skeletons.

After placing us in groups of four abreast, they chased us to an unknown destination with wild screams and whistling whips. We were leaving the station, and we were marching with a very quick pace. We were using the last bit of strength we had. Those who had packages with them threw them away just so they could keep up. If we could not keep up, as many could not, the punishment was quick and severe: a rifle shot to the head.

I could hear many shots from where we had left the adult men at the station, the group that was then following us. I did not want to be left in a ditch like a few others even though my legs were giving out. And though I was cold and wet from the rain, I was sweating a little. I knew I must go on if I didn't want to share the destiny of those left behind.

These Hitler beasts were kicking and hitting us with rifle butts and whips. They didn't allow us to help those who were weak; they continued to kick us in the head and kidneys. There was no time to look for a station sign back there, and I didn't see any signs along the way. We came to a fork in the road, and we were directed to the left.

Finally, we got out of the woods and saw a very small settlement. After we passed through this community of just a few houses in the town with no name, I noticed a large building surrounded with a high wall, festooned with coils of barbed wire in giant loops.

Once in a while one of us fell on the ground, and then we would hear the loud gunshots as they screamed. There were some very young German schoolboys watching as we were passing. They threw rocks at us even though our bodies were already covered with wounds from the beatings. The boys wore a swastika armband, and they called us Polish bandits, Polish dogs, pigs and even spit on us. Some of the boys ran up to us and kicked us.

We came upon a very large gate made of iron, and I noticed a sign on the right of the gate which read something like *Ahrbiten*. I couldn't read the whole thing. On the other side there was another sign that read *Hospital* and *Koncentrationslager*, but no name. The gates opened, and SS men shouted the commands, "Schnell! Schnell!"

Chapter 30

We marched through the gates to the hospital as best we could, prodded ceaselessly by the sting of the whip and the very real threat of an instant death. I looked around at the enclosure. There were four high walls made of stone. These did not seem to be completed, but they were topped off with coiled barb wire that gleamed in what remained of the sunlight.

As if these walls and cruel wire were not enough to keep us confined, the Germans had also set up an electrified fence. We could hear the hum as we passed. The dead birds that littered the ground below the wire inhibited us from trying to chance that wire.

At each corner of the compound was a guard tower with a large machine gun manned by an SS guard. In the middle of the compound was a high tower with a roof over it. Just below the roof was a high-powered reflector searchlight. Inside the compound, there were many wooden barracks. Each building had been numbered with German precision.

Not all of the buildings were made of wood; some were of old stone. They marched us till we stood in front of the largest of these stone buildings, and we were told to, "Halt!"

A man and a woman dressed in white lab coats came out of the building, holding clipboards. The man looked to be the one in charge, as he was the one the leader of the guards addressed in hushed tones.

One of the SS men counted us and signed a piece of paper. Our escort from the train station left, and the new band of SS Guards took over. Two more men dressed in white came out of the stone building to greet us. I noticed there was a disagreement between the medical people and the jack-booted SS guards. From what I could determine, the doctors were upset that so many of us had been killed on the way from the station.

I found out later that German universities were paying 150 Deutsch marks for each child or adult delivered to the medical staff—money paid to the SS officials in charge of delivering us. To my horror, I learned that some universities were performing autopsies on live people. Even though some doctors showed some mercy by drugging their victims first, most did not. I cannot even begin to imagine the people's agony as the doctors cut them to pieces to see how long they could live without certain organs. It was monstrously evil and has tormented my nightmares to this day.

We stood in the compound shivering from the cold while these creatures completed their satanic business. The sun had gone behind a cloud, and the wind was picking up again. I felt like fainting, but did not. We were all hungry and weak. Some of us were burning up with fever, and none of us could remember the last time our thirsts had been quenched. Simply, we stood stripped of everything that we either knew or owned. We did not have names; we did not know who we were anymore or where we fit into the world. I was beginning to lose faith in God. If God were watching over me, why was He allowing this? I had no answer.

But though my faith was lagging, I kept trying my best to place my hand in the Lord's every second of the day; that was the only thing that kept me alive. In this place, death stalked us constantly, and to die was much much easier than living. I felt that I needed God to lighten my soul with something: a wish, a memory, a dream, a simple hope. But nothing came. I was alone and desolate in both my body and my soul. Instead of considering a future, I concentrated on living from one moment to the next. It was apparent that I could find my life taken from me at any moment. This had the effect of compressing time to an unbelievable extent. I felt that every minute took an eternity to pass; hours were simply beyond my understanding.

I tried to keep believing that I could find some sort of hope in this barren desolation. From past experience I knew that when I was going through this unbearable place, I had to be honest with God about my feelings. It had been a long time since my sense of humor worked. I used to think that there was humor in almost everything in life, and I used to rely on humor to get me through some difficult days. Now, the time had come when I had to live my life a minute at a time. Humorless. Was I Godless, too?

When I did finally allow myself to dream, I hung on to a slim hope that this was a mistake, a nightmare. When the dream was over, I realized how afraid I was. For a while there was a dreadful silence as my mind overwhelmed my senses, and I felt as though I were in a tunnel. The light was fading; the voices of the men disappeared and were replaced with nothing. I could feel my heart beating rapidly, and I started to swoon. I knew this could mean my death, and I concentrated and willed my heart to slow. As it slowed, I started feeling pain in my throat from both the Nazi's boot and the tail of the whip. I rubbed the marks self-consciously.

"You will march to building #2."

We did so, and when we arrived, he ordered, "Remove your clothing and leave it on the ground."

If there was a moment's hesitation from anyone, I did not see it. The constant volley of rifle shots killing those who had started this journey with us had convinced us to do whatever we were told without question. I stared at the people near me. All were as emaciated as I was, and all bore the marks of the Nazis: whip marks and angry bruises. Their skin appeared sallow and dreadfully pock-marked with healed bruises.

That day they made us stand outside of barracks #2 for nearly an hour. The sun was now gone completely, and the day was cold. I stood there trying to cover my privates with my hands, while I shivered uncontrollably. I wanted to be somewhere, anywhere other than here. Looking at the faces of the guards and those of the staff, I saw nothing but contempt.

They finally ordered us to go into the building. We were lined up, and our heads were shaved. The man who shaved mine used a razor that was very dull, and it felt like my hair was being pulled out by its roots. I did not cry out even though the pain was terrible. I gritted my teeth and held my screams.

When we were done, the guards began screaming orders to us in German. If we did not react or know what to do, the whip followed. If this failed to correct the people, they were shoved to the ground and their hands and feet were crushed under the guard's boots. The ominous cracking of their bones being crushed is a sound I will never forget.

We were then ordered to get into large cement tubs for a disinfecting bath. Two of the doctors and a woman in white came into the building while we were taking baths. They looked at us, naked and pitiful, and began laughing at us. They would go to the edge of the tub and place rubber gloves on their hands. Then they would begin touching us in our private areas and giggling. I was scared. The water smelled of disinfectant, and it was painful because of the open sores on my body. I said nothing.

During this ordeal, I started hearing those silent screams again. The feeling of hopelessness was overwhelming me, and I considered taking a run at the guards. I knew this would mean my death, but it would also mean the end of the pain.

Whatever they had in the water was burning my cut-up skin; I tried not to get in my eyes. These silent screams were forcing me to make a decision. One wrong move and my destiny would be the same as those poor souls we left behind on the way here from the train station. I was shaking from anger, and I gritted my teeth to keep my screams silent.

To my horror, I watched as the attendants would hold one of the children's heads underwater until he did not move anymore. Mostly they did this to the Jewish kids, but not exclusively. It was terrible to see them kill these boys, boys who had never done anything to them. Children who had loving parents and brothers and sisters, and at one time, teachers who cared for them. It was wrong, and it disgusted me to the marrow of my bones.

I will remember this painful bath forever. It seemed an eternity since we entered the water. We all were trying to keep our personal space, but it was impossible. Our naked bodies kept running into each other. I closed my eyes at times, trying to eliminate the oppressive reality. Other times I believed that the man was coming to hold my head underwater, releasing me from the agony of this world; it never happened.

Finally, they told us to get out. We stepped from the tubs, and the guards sprayed us with cold water from a hose. I was glad I survived the bath, but with the windows open it was very cold. They ordered us to get into ranks again, and they marched us outside and to the biggest barracks.

Inside of this large building, the space was divided into rooms with four beds and corridors. They gave us gray uniforms that had the letter "P" inside of a triangle, and they gave the Jewish boys the same uniforms with a Star of David. The material was paper-thin and felt like pajamas.

The Jewish kids, one gypsy boy, and I were separated from the other Polish kids. I think they put me with the Jewish children, because they somehow knew that my family was hiding Jews. Two men and a woman in white uniforms greeted us when we walked into the building. One of the men spoke fluent Polish, "This is a hospital, and we will make you all well. We have rules here, and you will follow them. You may not leave your room other than to go the bathroom or to the dining area. If you do, you will be shot. There is no escape. Anyone seen outside of the barracks will be killed."

Four of us were assigned to room #4. The doors were locked tightly, and an SS guard was posted outside of our room.

Chapter 31

Finding my bed, I lay down and tried to think. There had to be something good in this situation, but for the life of me I could not imagine what it was. The blonde guard outside our door was a handsome young man full of youth and possessing a comely appearance. But I later found out he was one of the chief sadists they called "enforcers."

The first couple of days were not as terrible as those that followed. Initially, we were allowed to use the restroom when we needed and had the freedom to walk to a cafeteria for our meager portions of food. This freedom eroded gradually.

The blonde guard and a woman with rough features named Helga would place us in our beds and restrain us for the doctors. The restraints were tightened on our wrists and ankles, and a strap was placed across our chests and made secure. When we were completely immobilized, the doctors would approach us and take blood from us for their own soldiers. Later they came with a hypodermic needle full of something and injected us—without saying a word. It seemed to me that they did not even think of us as patients, or even humans, but simply specimens for experimentation. They did not always inject us, sometimes they took a scalpel and cut the vein. They took a tourniquet and placed it tightly on the arm and stuck a rubber tube in the veins to collect the blood without anesthetic. I know that some bled to death during these procedures. I heard their dying screams.

Helga stood behind the doctors with a medical chart in her hand, taking notes. It was a dreadful time. Each new day brought on some loss of both my sense of identity and my viability as a person. I was weak, sick, and getting sicker.

In the midst of this, Helga would smile at me once in a while. I think she liked me; she gave me more bread and watery soup than the others. I guess I appreciated it. But it seemed to be of little import.

I knew that I was getting much more than the Jewish kids, but I could not do anything about that. I could see them when the door was opened, and they were deteriorating rapidly. It did not take a person experienced in the medical arts to tell, at a glance, that they were very sick. I recognized the signs of typhoid fever and other diseases. The very sick in our room and the adjoining rooms moaned and cried nearly constantly. No matter how ill they became, they were denied even the most primitive care and in a short time were dying. As I watched all that went on around me, I came to the conclusion that all of us would die, either from their medical "experiments" or from the abuse to which we were routinely subjected.

These daily injections made us so weak that I doubt I could have risen, even if I had not been restrained. I could hear the other children crying, screaming, and moaning. I could not stop myself, though I tried not to. I cried with them.

I was weary of seeing people dying. No matter how much I saw of it, I never got used to it. Hunger forced the inmates to try to escape. When they did, the machine guns would erupt, and they would die. I was told the man who did the shooting was rewarded with a couple of days off. It was hell on earth.

I wasn't feeling well; sometimes I couldn't stop shaking. I guess this was from the injections, but there was so much disease in this place I could not be sure. My mental abilities were diminishing as well. I was barely coherent at times. Other times, I think I was completely lost. I honestly cannot remember. Whole days I spent in this place have been wiped from my memory.

Physically I was ill, but the mental tiredness was even more debilitating. Between the crying and moaning, the injections and the sickness, I was getting to the point of complete mental exhaustion. Human suffering inside this barbed wire camp became an every day affair. My life at this time in this camp had no meaning to me. I was at the point of not caring if I lived or died. I felt as though my Lord had abandoned me, when I most needed his help.

All that I wanted was a small scrap of hope. I was trying desperately to hold onto whatever remnant of faith in the future and the goodness of God I had left. But it was extremely difficult. I can remember promising the Lord in prayer that if he would only lessen my pain, I would become a much better person. I was so desperate that I asked God if pain was my only reason for being born. While I prayed, I was so focused in my prayer and requests to God that I did not realize that, in spite of the straps restraining me, I had loosed them and was on my knees praying as my mother had taught me. But this was an illusion as well. I remained tightly restrained and subject to the whims of my captors.

When I was in the midst of this, Helga would begin to visit me without the other guard or the doctors. She would approach the bed with her eyes smiling mischievously. At first she would do nothing but look at me. But one day she removed the sheet covering my nakedness and began molesting me.

The situation was hopeless for me. Not only were the doctors doing their worst, this woman would come smiling and commit a form of rape on my restrained body. Apparently, she liked this as she started coming to me two or three times a day. I screamed when she came, but she would place her hand over my mouth or place the pillow there to silence my screams all the while saying, "Shhhh."

Every day that passed, I remembered less of my former

life. I think this was because of the drugs. For some reason I thought my eyesight was also failing. At night the light of the powerful searchlight would swing through the window. I could hear the terrifying screams of some poor soul who was being taken to surgery for experiments. Their voices, full of pain and terror, echoed in the stillness of the compound.

Though I lost track of time, the days continued to pass. The children who were held in this hospital were in dire circumstances, and every day they seemed to worsen. We were now so disease-ridden, that even the guards would not venture into the rooms without wearing gloves and surgical masks. Many of us were dying; every day some were being transported to universities, and more were simply removed from the room.

As I had been told, those who were very close to death would have the bottom of a foot sliced by either a doctor or the enforcer; then they would be pulled to the end of the bed so their feet would hang over the bucket placed at the end of the bed. They would then quietly bleed to death.

Outside of this building there was a huge shallow dumpster, and every day they carried the kids who had died or were dying and threw them in the dumpster. Some of the kids were still alive when they were thrown into the dumpster. The SS men would climb into the dumpster and step on their necks, kick their heads, or stomp on their ribs with their boots until they stopped moving. At the end of the day, a tractor came and hauled the dumpster away to be emptied. I witnessed these things through an open door.

One season seemed to bleed into another; it was getting very cold out now. The blonde enforcer would leave the windows open so that it was deathly cold in the room. We were all freezing. Those of us in precarious health would develop pneumonia. Some died nearly every night.

Apparently, they had nearly exhausted their store of diseases to inject us with because the focus of their experiments changed. They would take us into a darkened room and leave us there. After several hours passed, they would come in and quickly examine our eyes. I am not sure what they were looking for; I only know that the light the doctors used hurt my eyes terribly.

Sometimes, when we were placed in the dark room, the temperature would begin dropping. I was so cold that I believed I would never get warm. I tried to keep myself awake, but eventually I would succumb, as we all did, and pass out. After we were all unconscious, they would remove us from the room and bring us to consciousness. It was an abominable torture, and there was nothing we could do about it. Well, there was one thing, but I was not yet ready to die.

In the distance, I could still hear things. I could hear the machine guns spitting death into the night. Once, from my room, I saw a man nearly cut in half by the hail of machine gun bullets as he tried to make for the wall surrounding this place. I don't believe he wanted to escape. I believe he wanted to die.

I also can recall hearing bombing; maybe it was the Russian planes bombing targets almost every day. It seemed as though the bombs were falling close to the compound. But they did not hit the compound for some reason. I used to pray that the bombers would bomb this camp.

They fed us poorly. Our food consisted of a small piece of crusty bread and some watery soup. I was so hungry that I could eat it in seconds. They did not give us utensils to eat with; instead I would eat the bread and drink the soup. If a clump of something remained in the bottom of the soup bowl, I would scoop it up with my fingers. Someone said that sometimes the soup was made from ground human bones. I did not know if this were true, but I knew that things were changing within me. I had nearly lost my appetite, I was drugged most of the time, and I was in constant pain. As sick as I was, I tried my best to eat and pretend that I was fine. The alternative was the man cutting your foot with the scalpel and bleeding to death. I did not want to end up in that fatal dumpster. I pretended that everything was fine.

The next morning, I was awakened by the sounds of dogs growling and barking madly. I turned my head toward the open door and saw a sight I can never forget. A Jewish man, I did not know his name but remembered him because he had given me extra food in the cafeteria area when I first arrived at the compound, was on the ground, and the blonde SS guard was kicking him repeatedly. The man's crime was to try to take some of the food the dogs had left in their dishes. The blonde man was cursing him and kicking him viciously. When the man passed out, the enforcer released the dogs. They attacked the man wildly, ripping pieces of his flesh from his body and eating them. The dogs were getting more and more brutal, and finally one of them ripped the man's throat open, and he began bleeding profusely. Blood was spurting everywhere, and the dogs were licking it up as fast as it came. I started shaking in my bed. I felt so sorry for the man; he seemed to be a decent fellow. His crime of being hungry was not worthy of this brutal death.

The silent screams came again. They were with me nearly constantly now. I tried to think that it was God's will that this man was killed in such a manner. But if God intended to end this man's suffering, why did it have to be in such a heartless way? I had no answers.

I knew that only a few of us who had come on the transport were left alive. But every day new children were brought to take their places. Though most of my contemporaries were dead, the population of victims in this camp was increasing.

Half groggy and confused, I dozed off when night came.

The next thing I remember was when I felt my legs being pulled toward the end of the bed. I saw the blonde guard coming toward me with a scalpel and dragging a bucket. I watched to see if he would go to some other bed; he did not. When he viciously sliced the bottom of my right foot, I knew that my time was up. I did not want to die here. My family would not even know where I was buried. I forced a smile and looked at the man. His expressionless face showed no emotion. When he left, I began to pray harder than I ever had.

Chapter 32

After I was done praying, I tried to think of a way to get loose. My hands were restrained by leather cuffs to the sides of the bed, so I began thrashing around wildly in hope of loosening the bonds restraining me. I knew I did not want to die like this. If I had to die, I wanted to die for something. But all of my thrashing only served to accelerate the blood flow from my foot. The bottom of my right foot felt warm, and the blood drained out of me faster; I could hear it drip into the bucket.

I was silently screaming in my mind and doing everything I could to get loose. Suddenly there was the sound of many explosions. These explosions were not in the distance; they were right here. The building rocked wildly in response to the blasts. In between the explosions, I heard the sounds of automatic gunfire. At this moment the door to my room burst open, and Helga came running in carrying a big knife and a bag.

She took the knife and quickly cut the straps that were holding my feet. She reached into the bag and retrieved a long white rag and wrapped it around my right foot tightly. Moving up the bed she cut the remaining straps holding me in bed. Without communicating, she retrieved a pair of pants and warm jacket from the bag. She put the pants on me and tightened a belt to hold them up because they were too large. Retrieving a pair of boots, she forced my feet into them and helped me from the bed.

When I stepped on the floor, I could hardly move. She pulled me along to the open door. We stopped at the doorway and looked. I could see that one of the buildings was on fire.

The watchtower with the searchlight had been knocked down, and people were running everywhere. Everyone was searching for a place of shelter away from the hail of bullets. The camp was in chaos. Helga thought for a moment and then pulled me along.

She looked toward the main gate, which lay in ruins because of the bombs, and headed that way. The thick bars of the gate were twisted and wrecked. They looked like pretzels in the wan half-light coming from the rising sun and the remains of the light fixtures. I knew Helga was trying to run to the trees, but I was slowing her down. I felt badly about this.

We continued moving toward the gate, and when we were almost there, the blonde guard started yelling, "Halt! Halt! Or I will shoot." We did not stop, but kept moving as quickly as we could toward the gate and the forest beyond. He took his pistol and began firing toward us. Helga was hit and fell to the ground. She screamed, "Keep going, Mitch; you can make it!" The blonde SS man took his gun and leveled it at me. At that moment an army vehicle was backing up really fast and ran him over. His gun fired aimlessly into the air as he was crushed.

In a weakened stupor, I kept moving. I entered the forest and tried to get as far away from that camp as fast as I could. By the time I was clear of the compound, the sun had risen. As I slowly walked through the forest, I thought, "This is a beautiful sunny day." But it was cold. The good thing was that after walking for a while, I felt my appetite return. If only I would have had something to eat—

While I was in that camp, I had completely lost track of time. I did not even know what month it was. I knew it was nearly winter when I entered. Even more importantly, I had no idea of where I was. I felt I should go east, but I did not know why. I was still disoriented from the drugs, and it seemed a good direction. Perhaps I could meet up with the invading Russian army this way. There were some narrow paths in the forest that I followed. When I was going down a hill, I saw a small stream up ahead. As I was very thirsty, I made for the stream. I looked around when I came to the opening just to make sure it was safe. When I saw nothing, I drank my fill of the cold, clear water. It was wonderful.

I walked for hours, trying at every turn to keep away from the main roads where I might meet the German army. Sometimes, I would come out to the edge of the forest to see if there was a house or a farm located nearby. I did not know if I was in Russia, Poland or Germany. This information would have helped me decide what to do.

The longer I walked, the slower I moved. Sporadically, I could see Russian fighter jets come down looking for Germans. When they did not see them, they flew higher to continue the search. I followed the stream as long as it allowed, but the path was moving away from the stream. As I ventured to the water to get one more drink, I sat on a big log and tried to think. I was sick, tired, lost, and hungry. I was trying desperately to place my hand in God's, hoping for his guidance. In my situation, I knew I needed a miracle to survive.

I was so cold that I was shivering uncontrollably. It seemed like I had been sleepwalking away from the camp. When I had started into the woods, the ground was red with my blood wherever I stepped. I was afraid that I would bleed to death. Now, I was afraid of dying from exposure.

My thoughts shifted to the bombing of the camp. It was a good thing that it was destroyed, but I felt badly about Helga. Though I had learned to hate her, she had given her life so that I might escape. That was an important and selfless thing to do. I simply could not understand why she did this—even though I was grateful for that one merciful decision. But her actions helped to restore my faith in human beings, at least a little.

Her decision also nourished my own feeble will to survive at that moment in time. It did not seem fair of me not to try my hardest, considering that she had died giving me the chance. It was soon cold and dark, but I kept moving. I needed food badly, and I needed shelter. I knew that without one or the other, this was probably my last night.

I did see a rabbit a couple of times, but I was in no shape to try and catch one. I looked for edible roots but could find none. I did not see any fish in the stream, although I believed they were there. But again, I had no way of catching them. I also remembered that there were wild boars in the woods of Poland, if that is where I was. I honestly did not know.

My situation was desperate and becoming more so. Yet, I was happy that I was free, particularly when I considered the alternative—helplessly restrained and bleeding to death. I kept walking slowly. I had noticed, some time ago, that the cut on my foot had stopped bleeding. But it was nearly dark, and I needed shelter. Food was out of the question at this time; I was simply too weak to look for any.

I went down the stream and got another drink. While rising from the water, I saw some haystacks in a small valley ahead of me. I was excited. Where there were haystacks, there would be a farm! I thanked God and kept moving my feet toward the haystacks. I knew that the haystack would provide some shelter, if I could only get there. I got close to the first one when I saw a house in the distance with smoke coming out of the chimney. However, I did not know if I was in Poland or Germany; I eliminated Russia since I saw the Russian fighter planes. Uncertain, I did not want to venture to the house at night. I burrowed into the hay as deeply as I could and pulled the hay around me. Before I allowed myself to go to sleep, I thanked God for sparing my life once again. I thought about my parents and my family as I prayed. I fell asleep.

My shivering woke me near morning. As I was trying to get myself reoriented, I remembered the house from the night before. I wanted to go there, but I was not sure if it was Polish or German. I figured that I would listen to see if they had a dog. If they had a dog, it was not a Polish house. Polish people were not allowed to keep dogs anymore.

I moved out of the hay. I wanted to sit and look at my foot, but I did not. It was too dark to see, and the snow was falling. It was simply not the right time or place to worry about it. I was still cold and weak and crawled back into the haystack to rest a while. I fell asleep again.

The next time I woke, I moved out of the haystack, and there were three men standing there. They were dressed in civilian clothes and one of them said, "What have we here? Come out, come out, boy." The fact that his words were in Polish set my heart soaring.

When I moved completely out of the haystack, I stumbled and fell. One of the men helped me up, "I'm sorry, I'm pretty weak. The Germans cut my foot."

"We know, we know. You were very lucky." The man said. "And we know all about the Germans."

"Who are you?"

"I am Captain, and this is my sergeant and private."

I looked at them. The fact that they did not offer their names was not surprising. In this crazy war, the less information that you knew, the better off you were. I knew this. I looked at them. The man introduced as Captain looked Polish; the other two looked Jewish.

"Am I in Poland?" I asked.

"Yes"

"I need to get to Baranowo, near Ostroleka."

"I know of these places," he said as he gestured. "But you're not in any shape to travel. Come here and let me take a look at your foot. It looks extremely painful."

They helped me to my feet. One of the Jewish men picked me up and carried me back into the forest where more men waiting. They then proceeded to carry me deeper into the woods. It was not that difficult a task; I was nothing but skin and bones. They brought me to an Underground bunker and went inside. He carried me down the stairs and placed me gently on a chair.

Chapter 33

The young Jewish man knelt before me and carefully removed my boot and looked at my foot. He sighed as he began unwrapping the bandage. The first layers came easily, but the blood had caked dry, and the white cloth, now stained maroon, refused to let go of my foot. Several of the men came over and looked. They agreed; it was infected. Taking some warm water, they bathed my foot until the bandage was released.

Another man brought me a large bowl of hot soup filled with delicious vegetables and some freshly cooked bacon. I was so hungry that I took the bowl and started drinking the soup so quickly that I began to choke. The man who brought it touched my shoulder and said, "Take it easy, son, we have lots of time here. And there is more, all you want. Besides, if you try to eat too fast, you'll be sick."

One of the Jewish men who had brought me from the field rolled my pants leg up and said, "Boy, you have a shrapnel cut in your leg." I did not know I had been wounded. In truth, I honestly had not felt it. Pain has a way of masking more pain. There is only so much pain our minds are capable of assimilating, and I had gone beyond this point.

Just as he said that, a tall slender lady with blonde hair walked down the stairs into the bunker. She was carrying a bag over her shoulder. When she saw me, she rushed to my side, looked at me, smiled and said, "My poor child." She placed her bag on the floor of the bunker and began rummaging through it. She brought out a lot of things I was not familiar with and placed them carefully on the edge of the bed. She then washed the bottom of my foot with some liquid that burned a little. "This will hurt; I am sorry. But it is necessary for you to get well." I did not speak; I merely nodded that I understood. She finished cleaning the wound and carefully applied some salve. Taking some clean bandages, she wrapped my foot carefully. After finishing with my foot, she addressed the shrapnel wound in my leg. "This is only a flesh wound. Let me clean it and wrap it; it should be fine." She smiled. "You know your foot is infected, don't you?" She asked.

I nodded. "The men told me."

"Just stay off it for a couple of days. I have cleaned it and disinfected it. It should heal nicely now. But you have to stay off of it. Do you understand?"

"Yes, thank you."

"Here's some aspirin for pain. Take two now and save the rest for later."

"Thank you." I took the pills and slept for a long time. Probably the entire day, though it was very difficult to tell day from night in the bunker. Without any windows, the days and nights melted together.

When I awoke, I was bathed in sweat, although I felt a lot better. My foot still hurt me terribly, but not as much as it had before. The young Jewish man brought me two aspirins, and I took them. He also brought me some more warm soup and a slice of fresh bread. The people here were taking good care of me, and I truly did appreciate it.

I thought about the fact that the hay I was sleeping on was clean and soft, and the blankets were nice and warm. And best of all, I am *free*! I nearly shouted the word aloud. Compared to the hell I had been living through, this was nearly heaven, and the people caring for me were angels.

But with all of the good they were doing, the questions about my family and my home continued to bother me. I missed my mom, Andrew, and Sophie. And I did not know what had happened to my father. As I slept, warm and secure in the bunker, I planned on when I could leave to begin the journey back to Baranowo and my home.

I intended to ask the captain tomorrow about leaving. If I felt better, I wanted to be on my way. I asked the Jewish man, "Is it day or night?"

"It's 11:00 PM."

"What's the weather like? I was thinking of starting for my home soon."

"It's cold, and we have about ten centimeters of fresh snow. You will need better boots, clothes that fit, and a hat if you are to have a chance of making it."

I sighed. I knew that I could not go now, so I relaxed on the bed. There were twelve men in the bunker now, and they included me in their conversations. While they had not introduced themselves, I did not find this unusual. There was still a war on. I listened to them talk as I drifted off to sleep again.

The nightmares returned. I had seen so much that these visions would not leave me alone. The doorway of the hospital kept opening and showing me things I did not want to see. Events like seeing that nice Jewish man ripped to pieces by the dog, German soldiers stomping the heads of babies in the dumpster, machine guns tearing a man to pieces as I watched—they were horrific, haunting images. As good as I felt, the nightmares robbed this good feeling from me. I was left sad and despairing with tears in my eyes as I slept.

The woman who had wrapped my foot woke me in the morning and said, "How are you feeling, my son?" Her smiling face and words thrilled me. It had been so long since I had seen anyone smiling or caring for another. And her calling me *son* made me feel...loved, I guess. I looked into her eyes and said, "I'm feeling much better, thank you. But I think I had better get ready to travel again. I need to find out about my family. The Nazis separated us. My father was in a different camp, and I am not sure how my mother and sister and brother are getting on."

"Yes, this war is terrible. We're all separated from our loved ones. Your fever is gone now. But before you eat again, I want to look at your wounds."

She carefully unwrapped my foot and examined it carefully; she did the same with the shrapnel wound in my leg. Finally she looked at the rest of my body. She noticed the myriad of puncture marks in my arms and said, "They really did a job on you, didn't they?"

"They were injecting me with something nearly every day. Stuff that made me lose my memory and worse, I don't know." I said as the tears formed again.

"Did any of the other children escape?"

"I think so. But when I left, the place was terribly confused. I'm sure that some got out, but I'm also sure that many did not."

"Listen, you are in no condition to travel. Perhaps in a couple of days."

Every day she came and examined me. Often she would take some sort of instrument out of her bag and look into my eyes. She also scraped some skin from my arms. "This is to look at under the microscope," she said.

I continued to get better, but I stayed in bed. They brought me food and water whenever I wanted it, and I was glad. I was very grateful for the blonde lady. I think she was a doctor or a nurse. I was not sure, but I was glad to be getting better.

One day she came carrying a sack and placed it by my bed. "What is in the sack?" I asked.

"Clothes: boots, a jacket, and a hat for when you are feeling better." Just before she left, she placed her hand on my head and spoke very seriously, "I think you should stay here for a few days yet. You need to get stronger. Look at you; you're nothing but a living skeleton. We need to put some meat on those bones. As for your family, don't worry so much. They are probably free by now and looking for you. This crazy war—" she said in disgust. "But I will see you tomorrow."

I dressed in the clothes and sat on the bed. The young Jewish man came over to me when she had left and said, "Look at you. With those clothes you could be one of us. Perhaps if you had a moustache." He grinned. He was always smiling, and that made me feel better. I knew that his parents had been killed at Auschwitz, and I said, "I'm sorry you lost your parents. Is there anyone else in your family?"

"The Underground is my family now. But after the war, I would like to go to America. It's too crazy around here. No, I think America would be better."

I liked him. He was a warm person, and his constant jokes helped me immensely. I even felt my own sense of humor ebbing back slowly. Perhaps, it never would come back completely. I had seen so much that I was not sure if I could ever be the same person I was before.

It had been over two weeks since I first entered the bunker. I could now walk pretty well, and my limp was almost gone. One morning, very early, the woman came again, "If you still want to go, today is the day."

"I'd like that."

"We will have to travel through the forest. The captain and I will go with you until we can point you in the right direction. But first let's have some breakfast."

She brought me a long coat and some homemade gloves. I tried them on, and they fit me just fine. She then brought a bowl of hot kasza to me, and I ate it all. I did not know what my next meal would consist of, so I wanted to eat while I had the chance.

These people had been wonderful to me, and I would miss

them. They had surely saved my life. The blonde lady who healed me and the young Jewish man with the fantastic sense of fun still occupy a warm place in my heart. The young man in particular. I have thought about him a lot and have come to the conclusion that he must be made of steel. To lose your family and still have enough humanity left to help others shows a remarkable inner strength, which was something that I appreciated. He would smile often and easily, but if you looked into his eyes, you could see the pain there. I guess it was something we all had.

Some of the men came over and shook my hand and wished me luck, saying, "God be with you."

The young Jewish man came to me and said, "Hey, we'll see each other again. Perhaps in America."

"I'd like that." I replied.

I walked out of the bunker into the sunlight.

Chapter 34

The day was bright and sunny as we walked. We knew that it would make it easier for the Germans to see us, but we also knew that it would make it easier for the Russian planes to see them. We decided to risk it.

We walked down a narrow road leading away from the bunker. At the bottom there was a horse and wagon. "That's for us," she said. The captain helped me to get up on the wagon, and they both sat in front with the driver. We traveled through the forest for a long time. When we came to the edge, the woman said, "This is as far as we can go."

I jumped off the wagon; the captain and the woman did as well. She fastened my coat collar and pulled the hat down to cover my ears. She told me, "You'll have to follow this road the best you can. If I were you, I would travel in the forest as much as possible. It will be more difficult for the Germans to see you."

"I know." I smiled. I had been doing this sort of thing for years now.

"About twenty kilometers from here, there is a village. After that one, there is one more on this road, and then you'll be in Baranowo. When you travel, ask the local people where the Germans are. They'll help you get to your home. When you get near to Baranowo, you will hear artillery shells being launched from the Russian side of the river. Don't be overly concerned. The river is not frozen, and the Russians will not cross it yet. Besides, the Russian army is in no hurry to help the Polish army. They have not helped us before, and they will not now."

The woman hugged me and the captain patted my head

and said, "Go with God."

I returned the hug and thanked them both for their kindness and for saving my life. "I'm sorry to go. I really am. But I have to find out about my family."

They said that they knew and smiled as I walked away. I glanced back to see the wagon turning around to bring them back to the bunker. I was on my own and walking toward my home. I went from the forest into an open field with an occasional clump of trees amidst the rolling hills. There was a road winding its way through the hills, just as the woman doctor had described. I warily followed the road.

As I walked, I considered that I had not seen my family in a long time. To tell the truth, I did not know how long it had been. It was wonderful walking toward home. Every step I took brought me closer to them. But the memories of what I had been through leaped into my mind. Two different labor camps, the last one worse than the first. The hell-hole where they were so cruel to us; all of these things vied for precedence in my mind. I kept my feet moving as I remembered.

The children who came on the transport with me to the frightful hospital were mostly dead. I knew that. I am guessing that at least 80 percent of them were killed—no, murdered—before the camp was overrun. Who knows what these injections were? I thought. I remember some people simply ending it by asking for a bullet.

At one time I could not understand this. I had been brought up in the Catholic Church, and committing suicide was considered a grievous sin. But time and experience have a way of showing us the answers to questions, even if we do not want to know these answers. I had been to that place in my mind where they had been. It was the place where pain overwhelms all. The pain of being alone. The pain of hunger. And, the desolation of the soul that this war has brought on. Many times, I thought of running at the German soldiers and allowing them to kill me. The pain infected a person in a way that is almost indescribable. It permeates your being until there is nothing left of the person but the pain. When you rushed into the hail of bullets then, what were you killing?

It seemed as though I had been walking for hours. My foot was not completely healed, and it started to hurt terribly. While I was doing much better than I had been before entering the bunker, I was still not completely recovered. I came to a bridge. After a moment, I remembered; I had crossed this bridge many times before. This thought strengthened me, for I knew that I was getting closer to my home.

There were trees on both sides of the road, and I stopped to rest and eat a little. The woman had packed some food for me. I ate a piece of the bread and drank some water. I remembered what it felt like to be hungry.

I continued on my journey of hope. I was wary of the Germans, but I was anxious to see my parents, Andrew, and Sophie. The eagerness brought on by walking in familiar settings was exhilarating. To the east, in the direction that I was walking, I could hear the artillery shells exploding. But that was some distance from me. Coming to the town of Orzel, I saw the house of a family friend, the Bocians. My father and I used to stop in here to visit with them. I knew that my dad and Mr. Bocian were good friends. I knocked on the door.

Mrs. Bocian answered right away. "Come in, come in," she said when she saw me. I could tell she did not recognize me. As I entered the house, I said, "Mrs. Bocian, I am Mitch Garwolinski."

"My goodness! Come here." She wrapped me in her arms and held me close. It felt wonderful. "Where have you been, Mitchell? Your parents have been worried sick about you." I could hear the frustration in her voice.

"The Germans had me. But I escaped. Are my parents okay?"

"Yes. Your mother has been worried about you, and your father has been searching everywhere for you. They are in your old house. They just found each other a month ago. Come and sit down though; I will make you some food. You must be hungry."

"I am."

She ushered me to a chair by the warm stove and busied herself in the kitchen. She was making potato soup. Soon the house smelled wonderfully. "Where is Steve?" I asked. Steve was their son. He was quite a bit older than me, but I knew him.

"The Germans killed him," she said as she softly whimpered.

"Why?"

"They said he was a sympathizer with the Polish Underground, but he was not. No more than anyone else had been." The tears fell as she poured some soup into a bowl and placed it on the table. "Eat, eat," she said. "Placek and the Gestapo came one night. They parked their car where we could not hear it. They knocked at the door. Steve saw them and tried to go out the back. Placek was waiting. He shot my only son!" The tears fell in earnest then. I tried to think of something to say, but I knew that there was nothing I could say to ease that pain. Nothing. We had all lost so much, but what words of comfort are there for one who has watched her only child being killed?

The potato soup was tasty and hot. I ate and listened as she talked. "The Nazis are terrible. The things they are doing are just evil."

"I know." I said with conviction.

She continued telling me stories of their atrocities. I thought of relating some of my experiences, but I did not. I could tell she was still grieving deeply and had her own problems. I listened to her and nodded sympathetically. She talked for some time about them and then said, "My husband is gone for a couple of days. If he were home, he could take you home tomorrow. But for now, please sleep in Steve's bed. I know you must be tired."

"I am. I've been walking all day."

She took me to a small room. When she opened the door, I saw how clean the room was. She turned down the bed and motioned for me to lie down. She walked away, and I closed my eyes in prayer. I wanted to kneel by the side of the bed as I had so many times before when I was younger, but I was too tired. I thanked the Lord for bringing me this close to home, for keeping my family safe, and begged him to grant Mrs. Bocian peace. Just as I closed my eyes to go to sleep, I heard the artillery in the east and grimaced. But in this room, the only noise was the ticking of the clock. It made me feel secure, and I slept.

My sleep was troubled again by the blonde SS man watching as the Jewish man was being attacked by the dogs. I thought of Helga. I thought of Steve. I finally fell asleep and did not wake until nearly 9:00 AM the next morning.

I got out of bed and looked out of the window at the sky. It was overcast and gray. I knew that there would not be any Russian planes flying today. That would make the Germans more free to move about. I walked into the kitchen and Mrs. Bocian said, "Good morning. How did you sleep?"

"Good. And long." I added with a smile.

"Come and sit down, I will make you some breakfast. But first I want you to wash up a little."

She strung a blanket across part of the kitchen. I stripped to the waist and washed myself with the warm water in a basin. Mrs Bocian brought me clean underwear and a shirt. "These belonged to Steve. You might as well use them," she said, her voice tinged with sadness.

While I was washing, I examined my wounds. The

shrapnel wound was healed and did not hurt any more. The skin over the slice on my foot was healed as well, but it was still sore from walking. All the time I was behind the blanket, she was telling me the news. "The Russians are pushing the Germans back further each day. But those who are still around are more evil than ever. You must avoid them. Do you understand?"

"Yes, Ma'am, I do."

I dressed quickly and came out from behind the blanket. She had placed a bowl of cereal and a stack of potato pancakes on a table with a long bench. I sat and ate. It was delicious. "How do you like the potato pancakes? My son Steve used to love them. I made them for him all of the time," she said in a pained voice.

I was a mere boy, but I understood grief. I said nothing other than, "They are wonderful." She smiled. "Do you want any more, Mitch?"

"No, six is my limit," I said honestly.

She put the remaining pancakes in my shoulder bag, and I dressed in my hat, coat, and gloves and headed for the door. She hugged me warmly, her eyes glistening, and said, "Be careful! And go with God."

"God bless you, Mrs. Bocian. And thank you so much."

I walked out of the door into the cold morning.

Chapter 35

As I came out into the elements, I realized that it was much colder than it had been yesterday. The road was straight, and there were tracks in the middle of the road from both wagons and sleds that had already gone this way. I followed the tracks because the walking was easier. The alternative was to trudge through the thick snow. I was lucky as this road was used only occasionally by the local people.

To my right was a pine forest whose trees seemed to form a green river flowing majestically down the hill—the green boughs were crowned with white snow. Houses lined the road on both sides, but I did not see much activity in them. It was comforting to know that I was getting closer to home. I continued on this road until I reached the main road. Then I had to make a decision. If I took the main road, there was a good chance that I would encounter German troops and the Gestapo. But the other way was clogged with snow. I decided to cross the road and head for Poswience, a rural part of Barnawo—and stop by my aunt and uncle's house before going home.

The old road I had been traveling on continued past the main road, but the tracks from the wagon and sleds were now gone. I made my way along the road, walking at the edge of the pine forest through the thick snow. It was difficult walking; I struggled mightily. Finally, I came into the outskirts of Poswiencie, almost parallel to the church.

My mind was racing. The closer I got to Baranowo, the more I thought of my experiences in this town, terrible experiences that had scarred me for life. But there was the other side of this as well. This was my home. This was where my family was. If I stopped by my uncle's house, I could ask some questions, and I had to be sharp before venturing further. At this moment, I did not feel I was. I was tired from the walking. Terrible visions of this town were filling my mind. I tried to put my hand in the Lord's for guidance, as my mother had taught me. I longed to surrender myself to God, but it was difficult. So many things had happened that drove a wedge between us.

When I reached the church, I moved quietly behind it. The bells were ringing, calling the people to mass. In the distance, interspersed with the clarion call of the church, were the almost incessant explosions of the Russian artillery shells. When I crossed the main street, I witnessed the Nazis moving about. I saw a German car cross the cemetery, knocking over gravestones as it went. It seemed like the Germans were all over the town—scattering as if they were maggots exposed to the sunlight. I saw my uncle working in the barn. I approached the house and knocked softly.

You have to remember that my "aunt" and "uncle" were really cousins. But they were close to my family and had always treated me as if I were a part of their family. When my aunt opened the door, I looked at her. She was emaciated and drawn. She looked as though she had just come out of a concentration camp. When she saw me, she screamed with joy. She opened her arms and hugged and kissed me repeatedly.

She called for my uncle. He joined us immediately. "My God, child, you are nothing but skin and bones!" she said. I looked at her and thought the same of her. But I said nothing. They kept asking me questions. I answered them as best I could.

She made me some cereal and told me, "Your parents have been so worried about you. Your father has been searching for you everywhere."

As she said this, a German staff car filled with SS men

pulled up in front. The men got out and burst into the house. "Why aren't you working today?" they demanded of my uncle. My uncle said nothing; the men forced the three of us out of the house. They pulled their weapons and shot my aunt and uncle in the head. They fell in a heap. When I ran to their aid, one of the soldiers took his rifle and viciously hit me in the head with the butt. I fell in a heap next to my dead relatives.

When I regained consciousness, there were a few women and a couple of men standing around. The SS men were gone, and the woman came over and bent over me. "Thank God. You're alive!" she said. The Germans had left me for dead. But I was still alive, if only barely. Two of the men carried me to one of the neighbor's houses. The woman washed the blood from my head and examined me. I was in bad shape. I could hardly see as my eye was swelling shut and filled with blood.

While they were caring for me, I asked, "What about my aunt and uncle?"

"Both dead," she replied. I felt an awful, crushing burden. They were people who had been very close to my family and me. One of the men asked, "Who are you, boy?"

"Mitch Garwolinski."

"My God! You are Mitch! Your parents have been searching for you everywhere. We have to let them know you are here. But it is hard to cross town. The Germans are more brutal than ever. Why don't you stay here for a while, and we'll get word to them?"

I was in no condition to argue. My head and eye ached, and I needed rest badly. There were no doctors around, so the people cared for me as they were able. She wrapped my head with a white cloth and covered my left eye. I was not doing very well. My mind was confused, I had no coordination, and

I was in terrible pain from the blow from the SS man.

I drifted in and out of consciousness. I don't believe I was sleeping. I was in a half-awake state with frequent nightmares. I kept having flashbacks from the camps, the hospital, and the brutal crime I had just witnessed. The death of my aunt and uncle devastated me. They were very close to me and had done nothing wrong. It was so difficult for me to overcome this that I felt like crawling into a hole and giving up. I realized that I was reaching a new level of suffering, and all I wanted was peace.

I stayed in that house for two weeks. The bandage had been removed from my eye. The eye remained bloodied, and though I could see through it, my vision was not nearly as acute as through my other eye. The swelling continued though, and I still felt sick.

In the middle of the night, at the end of this time, I felt someone's hand on me, and I awoke. It was my dad. He took me in his arms and held me close. Without saying a word, he held me for long moments. Finally, he asked, "Can you walk?"

"Yes, I can, Dad. Can we go home now?"

"Yes, your mother, brother, and sister are anxious to see you."

My dad helped me dress and put my boots on. I saw the man and woman who had been helping me standing near the doorway. My father shook the man's hand and then gave the lady a hug, "Thank you so much for taking care of Mitchell. There are no words...God bless you."

Outside it was dark with no moon. My dad said, "I have been waiting for this kind of night to come and get you. Finally, it arrived. Mitchell, we are going to have to go the long way around. Do you understand?"

"Yes. I just want to go home."

Taking my hand in his, he led me toward the barn. From

there we traveled around the cemetery and headed into the woods. "We are going to go around the cemetery and down by the river. I nodded that I understood and did my best to keep up with him. It was difficult for me as I was still groggy from the blow to the head, and I had a headache. When I could go no further, he picked me up and carried me.

We finally arrived at our home. My mother was awake but lying in bed waiting for us with Andrew, who was nearly asleep. She got up from the bed, and I could tell she was very pregnant. I rushed to her and hugged her and my brother tightly. It had been so long, and I had missed them so much. I doubt if the joy I felt at that moment has ever been duplicated in my life.

All those nights of medical torture, the deprivation and degradation I had gone through were always eased by the thought of someday going home. And now, here I was. I looked at my mother and said, "Mom, I saw my uncle and aunt—" She interrupted me with a hug: "I know. There was nothing you could have done. I'm so sorry that you saw that. But I am so glad to have you back." She embraced me again.

My dad helped me get undressed again, and he carefully placed me in my bed and covered me. Both of them hugged and kissed me before they retired for the evening. I was so excited about being home that I could hardly sleep. My mind was a tangle. All of the bad things I had witnessed were now interlocked with the joy I felt at being home.

When the morning came, Andrew came to my bed, and I hugged him. I had missed him so much; it was just great to see him again. He was almost five years old now. I always remember him following me around when he had been three or four. It was a pleasant memory. This served as counterpoint to the flashbacks to scenes of horror I had witnessed that seemed to manifest themselves both when I was sleeping and awake. I hoped that, in time, these would pass.

Chapter 36

I had been home for two weeks and was feeling much better. My foot no longer hurt, and the headaches had gradually diminished until they were mostly non-existent. The dreams and nightmares continued, but I was learning to live with them. My father explained it this way, "Son, you have seen things that would bother anyone. To be troubled by these things is normal. Just try to ignore them; they'll go away in time." I was not so sure, but I knew there was no alternative, so I just continued trying to live with them as best I could.

The weather had turned colder still. My father pulled me aside one morning and said, "Placek has left town. The man in charge now is the old fat man. But I think he will be leaving shortly as well." I felt better. Placek was a bad man. The old man was not one who ever gave anyone trouble. The Russian lines were moving closer to our home everyday. We could hear the beat of the artillery shells as they signaled the arrival of the Russian army.

While I was gone to the work camp and hospital, my father and some of the neighbors had built a bunker at the end of our property. They felt it was prudent to do so. The Russian planes were flying overhead everyday. The Germans certainly were not going to share their shelters with us, so we built our own.

My dad's sister, Czesia, who lived in the town next to the train station was supposed to be coming to live with us. She was going to bring her young daughter and my father's nephew, Slawek. Slawek's mother was Sophie, and the last we had seen of her was when she was on her way to a Russian prison. My father thought that his sister and the two children would be safer in Baranowo with us. Every day we watched for their arrival, but they did not come. I was looking forward to Slawek's coming. I liked him. Though he was a few years younger than me, we had a lot of fun together.

My dad asked me to go to their home and get them. He thought it would be safe, and he could not leave my mother and the young ones. I understood and left early in the morning. There were many members of the German army around, but very few members of the Gestapo. These beasts had all returned to Germany as nearly as we could tell. I traveled through the forest to their house. When I got there, the house was empty. One of the neighbors told me that they had already left.

I walked to the train station, thinking that I would get on the train to Baranowo for the return trip. When I came to the station, a train was just arriving. Unfortunately, so were two Russian fighters. They dove at the train spraying it with machinegun fire. Everyone in the area ran for shelter. The Germans had a bunker, but they were not the sharing type. I dove into a ditch.

The Russian fighters made a couple of passes and left. When the train pulled out of the station, I jumped on and rode it all the way to Jastrzabka. When I got off, I followed the forest paths back to Baranowo without incident. When I arrived, Aunt Czesia was already there with her daughter and Slawek. I was happy to see them, but I was very tired from the journey. I ate some supper and went to bed.

The next morning we began to move some provisions into the bunker. I was happy to have my brother following me around again. It made me feel important. Now, not only did I have Andrew, but I had Slawek as well. We carried the provisions to the bunker and then went back to the house for more.

Slawek was my Aunt Sophie's son. We had not heard

from Sophie in several years. We assumed that she was in prison, but we were not sure. Because of this, I felt sorry for him. But I did not know what to do, so I just tried to treat him in a special way. I was as nice as I could be to him. It seemed the least I could do.

About two weeks after Czesia and the two children had arrived, they left again. No one knew for sure where they had gone. We got up one day, and they were gone. The memory of them lasted much longer. But this war was a crazy thing, and it caused people to do strange things.

The noises from the fighting on the Eastern Front became more pronounced. The noise was now deafening. We knew the end was coming closer when my dad pointed out that the windmill between our house and the rest of the town was burning. He said, "The Germans are burning the windmill because they don't want the Russians to be able to use it as an observation post. I think they are burning some of the other buildings in town as well. I think it is time we move the rest of our provisions into the bunker."

The day was beautiful, but very cold. When most of the provisions had been moved, my father instructed, "Andrew and Mitchell, I want you to take these two geese to that clearing. At the clearing you will find two holes. Put a goose in each one and cover them with straw. If we survive the next day or two, at least we will have something to eat." We did as we were told. We found the clearing and the holes as he said we would. We put the geese into the holes and covered them. On our way back to the bunker, two Russian fighter planes came out of nowhere and began diving toward us. My brother got really scared. I did too. I pushed him down into a small ditch, and then I got on top of him to protect him. But the fighter just made one pass and left. We continued home.

When we got back to the bunker, an old man told us that the Germans had abandoned Baranowo. The main food supply store was being looted. I left Andrew in the bunker and ran to town. When I got there, everything was gone. I started back home.

There are two words in our language that have more power than any other words. They are not grandiose words with multiple levels of meaning. No, these are just small words with simple meanings. But these simple meanings can be positively devastating. Kingdoms have been lost, lovers separated, and people killed over them. The two words? *If only*. When applied in the context of real events, these words can have horrific consequences and alter the course of life forever.

If only the German people had not fallen prey to Hitler...

If only the Nazis had not harbored such deep prejudice against the Jewish people...

If only the soldiers had revolted against the evil...

If only the world had known the depths of its trenches...

If only their humanity and real religious values had triumphed...

The Russian artillery rounds were falling everywhere now. I saw some dead German soldiers on my way back. For some reason I went home by a different route than I usually did. The way I went was by a gentle sandy hill. In the summer going to this hill was like going to the beach. *If only...*

There were lots of weapons abandoned on the ground. I saw an automatic rifle like Sergeant Wagner had carried. I reached down and picked it up. It was a fine weapon. I checked to see if it had ammunition. It did. *If only* it had been empty. I carried it with me. *If only* I had left it there...

There were several holes dug in the sandy hill. These might have been good bunkers if they had been finished. But they were not. They were just holes in the sand. *If only* they had been finished...

As I walked, I saw a man with two small children, a boy and a girl, sitting in one of the holes. He had a rifle on his lap, and he eyed me suspiciously. *If only* he had spoken to me...

Suddenly the man leapt to his feet and put the rifle to his shoulder and pointed it at me. *If only* he had shouted a warning... *If only...*

When the man jumped up and fired, I instinctively returned the fire. The powerful burst of the automatic weapon from my small arms was accurate, and the three slumped to the ground. *If only* I had waited a moment...

When the shot missed me, I turned around. There was a German soldier who had his weapon out. The German had been aiming at me when the man fired his weapon, killing him and saving my life. *If only* I had understood!

I did not know what to do. I went to the hole and touched the children's faces. First the little girl, then the little boy. They were already cold. I felt an erupton of horror inside myself for what I had done. I got sick to my stomach and vomited on the hillside there. I did not want to harm anyone. It was not fair. Why had this happened to them? And me? *If only...*

I made my way back to our bunker in a daze. The rounds of artillery fire fell all around me. I ignored them. I continued walking, trying to sort out what had just happened. I remember walking down the steps to the bunker and my father grabbing my hand and pulling me down. He was yelling something, but I did not hear what it was. Not only had the battle come to us, but also I had a numbness inside of me and a dreadful roaring in my ears. It seemed as though I were underwater and he was trying to talk to me from the surface. I did not want to think about anything. I can remember that two German soldiers dropped into our bunker. One was shot in the foot and his friend was helping him. They did not bother us; instead they stayed for a few moments to catch their breath, and then the one who was not wounded said, "We have to go now." And they did.

Shortly after the German soldiers left, we saw the barrel of a different gun in the doorway, and a Russian soldier entered. He asked, "Are there any Germans in here?" We told him that there had been two, but they left. He stood for a while and then asked, "Is there any water?" My mother gave him some goat's milk. He drank it and took off his helmet. Though it was cold, he was sweating profusely.

The battle lasted a long time. Soon they started bringing wounded Russian soldiers into our bunker. Their doctor would care for them. If one of them died, they threw him out and pushed his body out of the way with the butts of their rifles. Many of the Russian soldiers died in this battle. The doctor who was treating the wounded was very kind, and he was talking with my dad. "When the war is over, Poland will get back the land the Germans have taken. And Russia will get back the land they lost in the last war."

One of the Russian soldiers came quickly into the bunker and told my dad to follow him. "One of the people from town has been seriously wounded when a round dropped through his roof. Maybe you can get him some help."

"I am not a doctor."

"I know, but we cannot get close to him. We do not speak Polish."

We walked through what used to be white snow. Instead of the purity of brightness that snow usually presents, we saw mud and blood and bodies lying everywhere. My father got a disgusted look on his face and turned to me and said, "Look, son, this is the face of war. Learn it and know it. It is not glory. It is death." I never forgot his words.

Chapter 37

The Russian soldier and my father were moving very quickly, and I was struggling to keep up. We had to jump over bodies that were strewn on the path. It was a horrific experience. I kept thinking that these men lying here were somebody's son or father. Somewhere, someone was waiting for them to come home—but they will not.

In a short amount of time, we arrived at the house. We entered the door and found the man right away. He was lying in a pool of blood. His stomach was ripped open from the shrapnel. He was unconscious now. My father and the soldier put the old man on a stretcher and carried him to his son's house and moved him into a bed. My dad made him as comfortable as possible, and we went to look for a Russian doctor. I doubted if we could find one or if the man would have the time to help the old man. We never found anyone to help. I assume the old man died.

We left and went back to the bunker. It was already dark when we arrived. With the darkness, the intensity of the fighting seemed to increase. It seemed to us that the German soldiers were mounting a counter-offensive and pushing the Russians back toward the river. I heard one man tell my father, "If the Germans come back, they will kill us all!" My father did not respond.

The bunker was now occupied by a completely different group of Russian soldiers. These were a much different group. There did not seem to be anyone in charge, and they were drinking vodka and shooting their pistols in the bunker, The drunker they got, the more dangerous they became. Some of the men started grabbing the women and taking them by force outside of the bunker and were raping them by the school. Somehow they missed my mother and Sophie. They were sleeping under a large goose-down comforter. They also neglected to find another eighteen-year-old woman. This girl was the daughter of one of my father's closest friends, a man who had been tortured to find my father and had given them no information.

After two hours of intense fighting, the war seemed to fade. By the morning, the war had passed us by to the west, and we could only hear the noise in the distance. The people began emerging from whatever shelter they had found. I followed my father out of the bunker as did my mother, Andrew, and Sophie. There were Russian trucks and wagons carrying the dead Russian soldiers away from their final battle. It had started out as a sunny day and the Russian fighters filled the sky. We could see the plumes of smoke in the air where the Russians had bombed German positions. In the afternoon, the sun faded behind the clouds, and the place took on a stillness I will not forget.

We moved back toward our home, although we could not enter as the Russians had taken it over. We went to a new barn my father had built and made ourselves as comfortable as possible. The barn was fairly warm as I remember it. I know that the Russians had slaughtered one of our goats and were eating it. In town, the big flour mill was still standing because the Germans had not had time to detonate the dynamite and anti-personnel mines they had placed. The Germans had also wired the small bridge to explode, but had not had time to do so. We had little to eat and our food supply for the rest of the winter had dwindled to practically nothing.

In a few days the Russians moved out of our house. Before they left, they broke the ice on the well and stripped to the waist in the snow and washed themselves. I remember this because it was terribly cold outside. I heard a man telling my father that they had found two little kids and their father in an unfinished bunker. They thought the Russians had killed them. I said nothing. I was becoming more and more morose as the time passed. When I heard the man telling of this incident, I felt like I was dead. My father noticed this and asked me many times what was wrong. I did not answer. The answer was too terrible to voice.

I kept having nightmares of the white sand. These dreams would find me whether I was sleeping or awake, and any stimulus could bring them on. White snow, white sand—all were there, condemning me for what I had done. I cannot emphasize enough how devastating this was to me. Literally, it changed my life forever. I still have the nightmares and keep speaking those damned words: *if only...*

Until that day, my utterances of "if only" always had to do with someone else—an individual, an army, a group, a force outside myself: *If only they...*

Then, my actions forced a shift in focus. It was no longer, *if only they....* It was now, *if only I...* Even though it was an accident, I was responsible. I was culpable. I was a part of the violence which had hurt others.

Within another month the town had formed a militia. The commander was a man whose wife had been raped and abused by the Russian soldiers. Russian Communists, who spoke perfect Polish, came into town recruiting people to join the Communist Party. The militia began rounding up the people they thought were German collaborators. Many people were falsely accused. There was an Underground army that was opposed to the Communists, and they would come at night to people who had joined the party and kill them. In the wake of the Germans, we found little peace.

It had been over a week since the war passed by us. We went to the hole where we had placed the geese, and by some miracle they had survived and were in fair condition. My mom hoped they would breed since there was a male and a female.

Sometime in May, we heard that the war with Germany had ended. But another war was beginning. This war was between the National army and Communists. My uncle Kuzia, who was also my Godfather, joined the Communists, and he and my father would argue frequently about whether my father should join the Communist Party. As I remember it, my father always won these arguments. My dad would tell him that he was simply against Communism. My father also added that he wanted to go the United States, and he did not want to do anything that would jeopardize taking his family with him.

Long after the war had ended, there were weapons and the detritus of war scattered on the ground nearly everywhere. Almost everyday someone would step on a forgotten land mine. I remember one incident in particular. A family with two small boys had both children killed on one day by stepping on abandoned mines. The father died three weeks later— everyone said of a broken heart.

The people and the militia collected the mines and dynamite from the big mill and the bridge and moved them about three hundred feet from the bridge alongside the river. We were told to stay away from that area as these were extremely dangerous.

One beautiful Sunday morning in the spring, my mom gave me some new pants she had made for me, and I went to church. My parents had gone to early mass, but I felt good in my new clothes. When I got there, I did not go in right away because some of the kids were playing behind the church like we used to do before the war. I went to join them. I remember, vividly, that one of the older boys—I think he was sixteen—

was trying to talk the kids to coming with him to the forest to see what kind of guns they could find lying around. He asked me if I wanted to go. I declined; after that terrible incident, I had lost my interest in guns. The area where he wanted to go was down by the river and the bridge. I watched them as they left. I went into church.

About forty minutes later, while the priest was giving his sermon, we heard the most tremendous explosion ever. The priest said, "I will cut this short." After the service, I followed everyone else down to the river. There was a cavernous crater from the explosion, and there were body parts lying everywhere. Nineteen kids were killed that day. The vision of the parents trying to identify an arm or a leg is something that I can never forget. It was an unequaled tragedy for my small town. Nineteen children!

I was glad that I had not gone with them, and I thanked the Lord for his guidance in shaping my destiny. Still, I was filled with sorrow for more senseless deaths and those poor families in the wake of that hateful war.

A couple of months earlier I had found a wonderful flare gun by a mill in the field. I had shot it a couple of times at night. It was like fireworks, and I liked it. I took the gun home and put it behind the furnace, out of the reach of Andrew. The gun had stayed in that position for two months without my touching it. Though I liked this gun, I wanted to have little to do with any gun.

I was twelve years old and still had not had a childhood. It seemed that there was always a responsibility for me. At age twelve I felt old and worn out. My father had changed, too. He seemed restless, nervous, and intolerant, not at all like he was before the war. I knew he was having trouble supporting our family and was trying, desperately, to bring the family to the United States. He was under tremendous pressure from friends who wanted him to join the National army to oppose the Communists. When he refused to join, they accused him of being a Communist. He was not.

My mother had asked the Red Cross to find my sister, Irene, and my Aunt Stasia. Sometime in June my sister and my aunt showed up at our house. I was so happy to see them. I hugged Irene tightly. All of the times when I had dreamed of having her return safely came true. It had been five years! I heard my aunt telling my mom that Irene and she had both been raped during the war. My sister had changed, but so had we all. My parents were understanding and sympathetic, and so was I.

Chapter 38

With the arrival of the spring and warm weather, there was another problem: the bodies. There were many bodies lying in the forest after the war. When I walked by them, the smell was incredibly bad. If I looked closely, the maggots were clearly visible. There were even more bodies floating in the river, the source of the town's water. Because of this, there was a typhus epidemic.

One spring day as I was bringing our cow back from the community pasture, I began feeling dizzy and lightheaded. About halfway back to our house, I lost consciousness. The cow, used to the journey, continued on without me. When it arrived at the house without me, my mom and dad began to search for me. When I woke up, I was in my bed with my parents taking turns placing cold compresses on my body.

I had developed typhoid fever. I was in good company; at least one out of three of us had it. The disease was not discriminatory; it infected both young and old. Our neighbors had already lost their children to the disease. I was scared because there was no doctor in town and no way to treat the disease.

I do not remember much about that experience. The only clear memory is of my mother cleaning and changing the bed regularly as I was constantly messing it up. She fed me by hand, prayed over me, and cared for me for three months. I was nothing but skin and bones by that time. I do remember one night in particular, because she was constantly waking me and placing cold compresses on my body. I had taken a turn for the worse, and I was not expected to survive. The fever was very high, and my mother sent for the priest to administer the Last Rites. I remember the priest coming there, but that is about all. The next morning when I woke up, my mom and dad were smiling. I asked, "Where are Irene, Andrew, and Sophie?"

"We sent them away because of your sickness. But you are going to get better now."

I did not respond; I simply went back to sleep. In a few days I got out of bed. When I stood, I could hear my bones rattling. My dad saw me trying to walk, and he ran to me and caught me before I fell. He helped me back into the bed and said, "Mitch, you are not ready to walk yet. But soon."

In three weeks time I was walking fairly well. My mother had gone into labor and gave birth to my brother, Steve. He was doing well, and I was happy. That evening, I walked to the middle of town where the kids gathered. It was getting dark, and I noticed that there were lots of the National army in town. Some people called them the "Underground," but this was different than the Underground that fought the Germans. They had captured my Uncle Kuzia and had him and another man who had joined the Communist Party and were beating them. While they were doing this, my uncle managed to get free and started running. A man shot him. He was not dead, but a woman came over and put a bullet in his head. The next day, when he was displayed in his casket, my dad took me with him to pay his last respects. Later, the Communists had a military funeral for him.

The town's militia was on the side of the National army, mostly because they were afraid of them. The so-called "underground" made one last attempt to enlist my father. He refused again for the same reason as before. He wanted to immigrate to the United States, and he would not do anything to jeopardize his chances. One night the men from the National army came and got my father and beat him badly with a long club. In the process they managed to break his arm and some ribs. Before they left, their leader said, "The next time we come, we will kill you."

"I am an American citizen. I don't belong to any organization, and I don't want to join one now. I am going to America." But his words fell on deaf ears.

Two weeks later, they framed my father and had him arrested. They said that he robbed a church. He did not, but they still took him to jail in a city named Przasnysz. While he was in jail, the town militia came and harassed my family, including the kids. We were eating supper when we noticed the militia commandant drinking with his men by a building that used to be a pharmacy. At this time it was simply a tavern.

The militia did whatever they wanted to and got away with it. They were supported by the Underground in case anyone would try to do something about them. I later learned that these were the same men who had framed my father by leaving bicycle tracks at our house. After we had gone to sleep that night, someone came and knocked on our door.

It was the militia commandant. He pushed the door open and came inside. In a drunken frenzy he pushed my mother against the wall and tried to force himself on her. I jumped out of bed and yelled, "Leave my mom alone!" He smacked me in the face and knocked me down. Pulling his revolver, he put it to my mom's chest and told her to get in the other room and to take off her clothing. What choice had she?

He put his gun away and was impatiently helping to strip the clothes off my mother—he was going to rape her. I had recovered enough, and I picked up a homemade stool that my dad had crafted a long time ago. I threw it at him. It knocked him down. I went to the main room and reached to the shelf above the furnace and retrieved the flare gun.

I returned to the bedroom and saw him reaching for his revolver. I aimed the flare gun and pulled the trigger. The flare hit him squarely in the stomach, and the force of the projectile knocked him through the window. When he was outside, the flare exploded into a shower of sparks. His stomach exploded while he was on the ground. He turned different colors, and the flare exploded again. I felt nothing, but went to help my mother.

My mother and I dressed and got Sophie, Andrew, Irene, and baby Steve and started walking through the forest to Jastrzabka. When we arrived, we knocked a the door of some friends. They were sympathetic and invited us in.

The next day they told my dad, who was still in jail, that they would not keep him any longer. They knew he had been framed, and, besides, he was in a Communist jail, and they cared little for the church.

After this last incident of harassment, my father sold our property in Baranowo and moved to a city named Wyszkow. Wyszkow was near to Warsaw and the American Embassy.

We made many, many trips to Warsaw. Often we went to the American Embassy, but other times we just went to see the sights. The city had been destroyed, but it was quickly being rebuilt. At the embassy, we were trying to take the necessary steps to immigrate to the United States. We stayed in this city for over a year waiting. Before we had our own home, we stayed with one of my dad's cousins. The city had a river named Bug that ran through it. We had a lot of fun swimming there and lounging around on the beach. From the window of our house, I could see the River Bug flowing and the white sand on the beach.

I was still having nightmares and flashbacks. I think the white beach sand triggered them. Finally, my dad came back from the American Embassy in Warsaw with big news. We were going to the United States. However, only Dad, Andrew, and I would be able to go right now. Mom and the rest of family would have to come later. Only those with birthdays before 1941 were allowed to leave. People born after that were not considered citizens. My mother would have to stay to care for Sophie and baby Steve. This seemed an imposition, but it was something that was policy at the time, so we accepted it.

My dad took me to the American Embassy in Warsaw often. I was getting more and more morose. He would tell me to, "Snap out of it." I did not. I could not remove the vision of the man and his two children that I had killed. It would not leave me alone.

I heard him say to mom one night, "I don't know what is wrong with Mitch. Since the Russian Front passed, he has this distant look in his eyes. I wish I knew what is wrong with him."

Finally the day came for our departure. It was difficult to say goodbye to Mom and the smaller children, but we knew it would only be a matter of time until they would join us. The three of us got a train at Wyszkow, and we headed for the seaport of Gdansk. We stayed in a huge building near the water and shipped out that day. We sailed on a ship named for the American war correspondent, Ernie Pyle.

I remember stopping at a German seaport and seeing the Germans, still in their uniforms with the eagle. Seeing that hated symbol unearthed too many bad memories. I tried to forget them though.

Later we went through a body of water—I think it was the English Channel—and then out to sea. It took us two weeks to cross the Atlantic. The seas got rough at times because it was late fall and nearly winter. Sailing on that ship was a new and exciting experience.

The best thing about the trip was the food. They gave us

bananas and oranges and cake, and so many other things that I had never seen before. Andrew and I thought we were in heaven. We spent every day walking the rails and watching for the first glimpse of America. We never did see it by ourselves. But we kept looking.

One morning my father woke us early, while it was still dark and led us to the side of the ship to see the lady with the lamp. He turned to us, and with tears in his eyes he said, "Now, you are free."

Epilogue

I needed to tell this story. Given the volative conditions in the world, I believe that people need to hear my story as much I need to tell it. If we listen and learn, perhaps something like this dreadful period in human history will never be repeated.

I am slowly making peace with myself and my situation. But healing is not always a timely companion. Was it necessary to endure the suffering, pain, and exhaustion of those war years? I do not know. I only know that courage is something that can be manifest in many ways. Perhaps in a way as simple as choosing to live rather than die.

I do not hate those people who did these things to me. But I have not forgiven them either. My therapist said the first step to recovery is to forgive. I am trying to forgive, but I also want justice. I would like to become a more loving and caring person. The experiences of my childhood left scars, so I am still learning.

For years my wife told me to take my coat off in the house; I told her that I left it on so I could get away quickly. It is very difficult to change habits that have been a part of your life since childhood. I believe that those who have not experienced what I was forced to live will never understand. My childhood was taken from me; that is something that can never be replaced.

It has been a long time since the war and I still have a wall around me. My spiritual life has helped me to accept what happened and to become closer to God. I have come to accept myself and realize that the things that I did, I did because of this faith. I know that I am an imperfect individual and I have done some things, which make my forgiveness difficult. But I know that the Lord loves me because I am His. And that is important.

I still keep searching for peace. As hard as it is to find, I have faith that it will come some day. I still have nightmares, although not as often. Sometimes, my smile only covers the tears and pain. When I am alone, I work constantly to channel my feelings away from hate and into a constructive energy that will make a positive difference.

I do still feel anger, anger for all the lost lives and all the suffering, anger because I lost so much time. My childhood was spent in the midst of meaningless violence, and this makes me want to cry. But I don't. Instead, I have dedicated myself to telling my story to any and all who will listen.

A few years ago I had an episode of aggressive prostate cancer that nearly killed me. I took radiation treatments and underwent chemotherapy. The cancer is now in remission. I am a marathoner, and the doctors tell me that being in such good shape helped me to beat the cancer. But facing death once more brought my feelings about my life to the forefront. I have rededicated myself to informing people about the Holocaust. I spend my time addressing groups of students about my experiences. From the first time I did this, I knew that this was what I was meant to do. It is clear to me that God has chosen me to serve as a living reminder to all that the Holocaust was real. The seeds of this hatred are buried within all of us, as are the seeds of love. It is our choice which seeds we plant and nurture.

Addressing high school students is difficult, but when I begin to tell them of my own survival, I can see them start to think and understand. In addition to speaking in schools, I spend significant time speaking in Synagogues in the Toledo and Southeastern Michigan area. The Holocaust is over with now, but discrimination and hatred continue with a vengeance. I do my best to make certain that I am always a valiant warrior in this battle. It is the least I can do for those who did not survive.

The most difficult thing to manage is my grief for my relatives, neighbors, my Jewish friends, and, of course, the father and his two children whose lives I took. Instead of just screaming silently, I feel like shouting for the world to hear. We must be on guard forever against this kind of tyranny, which threatens us both in corners of our hearts and in corners of the world. I am telling my story, not only because I am still angry, but because I believe that we have the power of choice over what kind of future the next generation inherits. When I used to walk by the mass graves, I could swear I heard babies crying. This emotion was too powerful for me and I always walked away. But we cannot walk away forever.

My father was a tremendous influence in my life; his kindness, generosity, bravery, and faith were foundational for me. He helped me become what I am and what I believe. There is a distinctive quality about people who have experienced such deprivation. He taught me to convert my suffering and anger into fuel to help others. That was a vital, timeless lesson. I am still trying to fulfill this directive though.

I had a therapist who helped me. She encouraged me to write down my experiences. When I told her about my sin of killing the man and his two children, she tried to convince me it was not my fault. She asked me if I normally go around killing people. I had to answer, no. She tried to convince me that killing them was not my fault. It was simply a tragic accident. But I still saw their faces everywhere I went. I did not know what to do. She finally wrote a piece of paper absolving me of my responsibility. She told me that when the flashback came, I should take out the paper and read it. I wore that paper out.

In writing this history, I was warned that doing so would

bring up the bad memories. But the story is important for people to understand. I still think of the Jewish woman who threw her baby out of the train car. I remember my aunt and uncle who were killed in front of me. But most of all I think of the man and his two children whom I killed. I feel guilty for surviving. I simply ask your understanding for my actions, and your perseverance in the defense of freedom and individual rights, so that such a thing can never happen again. Ever.

The terrible episode I described of *If only...* in my life serves as a constant reminder to me that I must always be willing to look within when I am ready to pass judgement. Although I have made some peace with myself, it is with deep humility that I share the impact of the lesson with you. Of all the *If only they...*moments we have, sometimes in faith we must probe, *If only I....*

I think too few of us are both cognizant of the dangers we represent to each other *and* willing to learn the skills essential for cultivating peace in this political, cultural, and economic chaos. Although the German Nazis perpetrated horrendous evil, frightful events cut from the same fabric have been duplicated from Rwanda to Cambodia and from the old Soviet Union to Iraq. The potential for one human being to do great injury to another is always with us. I, myself, will probably never fully understand the sights I saw along the road I've traveled.

The contrast between the joyless and oppressive existence I experienced during the war and coming to the United States still baffles me. In the United States, I found a community and country of good caring people. But, it has been difficult for me to integrate into this "normal society," where I don't always feel understood. I am different and changed forever by the violence and inhumanity.

I still believe in God and never doubt, not even for a

second, that my life has been a true blessing. I am reaching to the bottom of my soul and learning to love and laugh again. And although, as always, the road is long and hard, I will survive.

—Mother, Mary;
Father, Joseph;
Mitchell, Irene
About 1935

—Brother Andrew;
Mother, Mary;
Mitchell; Baby
sister, Sophie.
Taken in 1943,
during a 7-month
time of freedom
from hiding.

SILENT SCREAMS

—Mitchell's Mother, Mary. Taken after World War II in 1945.

—Canisters used in the death camps by the Nazis. Each canister held enough poison to kill thousands of people.

—Mitch Garwolinski, Sergeant First Class, during the Korean War. 1953

—Mitch at the memorial to child survivors of the Nazi concentration camps.

—Mitch at Bedford
High School in
Temperance, MI,
speaking to students.
November, 2001

—Mitch prior to
running a marathon
in Florida, 1998.

About the Authors

Mitch Garwolinski was a boy of seven, living in Poland, when World War ll broke out in September of 1939. His family was there, because his father, a US citizen, was working for the OSS (now the CIA). The turmoil of the war separated Mitch from his family for much of the next six years. During this time, he was captured and escaped from several labor and experimental camps, including Treblinka. With encouragement from others, Mitch wrote a journal of his war-time memories, which served as the basis of *Silent Screams of a Survivor*. He also devotes time to sharing his experiences with school and community groups.

After learning to run from the Nazis in the war, Mitch has continued to use running in long distance races as a coping mechanism throughout his life. He has run over 80 marathons, including Boston, and averages 40 races a year. Now in his seventies, Mitch continues to train for and participate in marathons.

In 1999 Mitch faced another hurdle: he was diagnosed with prostate cancer. However, like any other barrier he has confronted, Mitch fought back. He took the chemo and radiation, and the cancer presently is in remission. Mitch is a SURVIVOR many times over, and continues to be an inspiration.

෴

Bob Hoffman is a 54 year-old husband, father, teacher, and writer living in Muskegon, Michigan. During the last fifteen years, Bob has written numerous books. He believes that a successful writer is most often someone who has lived enough to put their thoughts in perspective. Bob has served on the advisory committees of many entities concerning the process of writing. His joy is in both writing and showing others how to capture their thoughts on paper. Bob has been married for thirty-two years to Yvonne and is the father of two sons: Lee, a twenty-year-old student at Michigan State University, and Chris, a sixteen-year-old sophomore in high school in Norton Shores.

Bob has written in many genres, including the techno-thriller, short stories, stories for young adults, children's stories, science fiction, literary fiction, non-fiction, philosophy and poetry.

A prolific writer, one of his current projects is a novel, *Challenge*, scheduled for publishing in 2005.